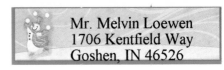
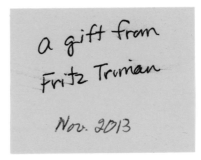

a gift from
Fritz Truman

Nov. 2013

Growing a Mustard Tree

By Matt Kirkas

The amazing story of Sundanese Muslims
coming to faith in Christ

D1495508

Growing a Mustard Tree

By Matt Kirkas

Email: matt.kirkas@yahoo.com

ISBN-13: 978-0-9893362-0-8
1. Missions. 2. Church planting.

Dedication

To my wife and children

Long periods of separation, trials and hardship have
been a part of your lives. Your love, sacrifice and
support throughout these years have gladdened my
heart and brought honor to our Father in Heaven.

To the wives and children of all the Sundanese
Christian Fellowship's church planters

Acknowledgment

Putting this book together would have been significantly more difficult if it was not for the help of Intan who transcribed all the interviews. Her enthusiasm for the Lord and His work is a beautiful testimony of how much the Indonesian Christians love God. Therefore I felt it appropriate to let you read the message Intan left me at the end of the transcription:

"The deepest desire of my heart is that the Lord, who Himself has begun this work among the Sundanese, who has left his footprints and handprints all around West Java, will complete this good work for the sake of His glory. May the Lord raise up among the Sundanese a new generation of disciples who take the Great Commission seriously—people of great faith, high intelligence and a deep regard for the Sundanese culture and history. The history of the ministry in West Java is His Story. He is the true pioneer, and He is the Master of the work among the Sundanese."

-Intan, August 2, 2011

May the Lord answer Intan's prayer.

Due to the sensitive nature of this ministry, proper names of people and locations have been changed.

The Parable of the Mustard Seed

"The kingdom of heaven is like a mustard seed, which a man took and planted in his field. Though it is the smallest of all seeds, yet when it grows, it is the largest of garden plants and becomes a tree, so that the birds come and perch in its branches."

Matthew 13:31-32

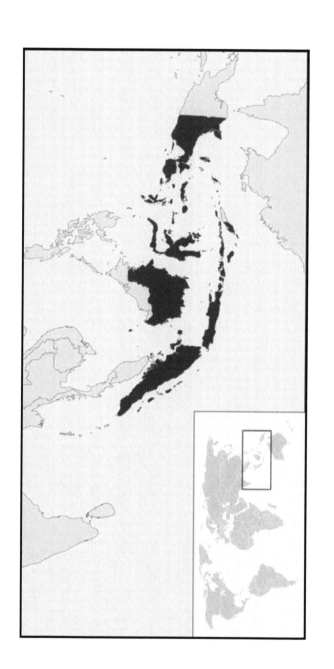

CHAPTER 1

Gathering the Seeds

For as long as I can remember, I have been curious about new places. I have always longed for adventures. How I wished I'd been born in the days of the pirates so I could sail the world in search of treasure! One Christmas, I received the wonderful gift of a globe. I spun it around and around, closed my eyes, and jabbed it to a stop with my finger. Opening my eyes, I proclaimed, "This is where I'm going to live!" I did it that first day, and I kept doing it, day after day, year after year. Never mind that more times than not my finger pointed to some spot in the ocean. It didn't matter. God had already placed a sense of adventure in my heart, and a desire to go anywhere He led me.

In college, where I wanted to go was on a short term mission trip to the Soviet Union (USSR). My parents said, "Absolutely not! You can't go to such a dangerous place!" I begged and pleaded and reasoned, but they would not relent. "You can go on a mission trip anywhere else," they told me. "Any place in the world except to a communist country."

"How about the other mission trip that's going to the Middle East?" I asked. "Can I go there?"

"Sure," they said. "That one should be safe enough."

How our perceptions of the world have changed in one generation!

It was on that "safe" trip that I first saw the great spiritual needs of Muslims. It was also on that trip that it became abundantly clear that I would never make a good "undercover" missionary. My big mouth would get me into way too much trouble.

On my college campus, I led a Bible Study for International Students. One fellow in the study came from Indonesia. I learned from him that despite the country having more Muslims than the entire Middle East and North Africa combined, Indonesia had a strong church community. This excited me. If I went there, I could minister alongside that church! This introduction, combined with my affinity for Asian cultures, convinced me of God's leading. I would serve the Lord in Indonesia.

But not right away.

My path took an unanticipated detour. For three years I worked as a computer engineer, pouring long hours into a project that was many years behind schedule. As frustrating as that was, I can now see that it was a season of preparation for me. The Lord was using my work experiences to teach me how to work in teams, and how to design and implement projects. These skills would be crucial to me in a few short years. My career path arched upwards as the company applied for four patents based on the software I had written for them. Yet my calling was clear. God was sending me to Indonesia.

The longer I stayed where I was, the more the comforts I was able to buy with my engineer's salary whittled away at my desire to leave. But God was teaching me another important lesson: Whatever the calling He places on a life, it cannot be negotiated. It must be forcibly acted upon. Once again, I set my mind on Indonesia. But this time I started making lifestyle changes that would prepare me for roughing it on the mission field.

Finally I went to my boss to tell him of my decision. As I stood in his doorway, the words poured out: "I've decided to resign. I'm moving to Indonesia to work as a missionary."

My shocked boss stared at me. "Come in," he said. "Sit down." He informed me that he had just prepared an offer for me and had it ready on his desk. It was a promotion and a raise.

"No, thank you," I said as politely as I could. "I have made my decision."

My boss never did understand, but he did accept my resignation. The world never seems able to understand, but it respects us when we act upon our convictions.

I started through the usual procedures—joining a mission agency, enrolling in seminary, and beginning a formal preparation program. As I studied, I also gained cross-cultural experience by working with an Hispanic church. The mission pastor and I wrote to various organizations, but with no success. One by one the Lord seemed to be closing the doors. I felt strongly that God wanted me to go to Jakarta as a self-supporting missionary, but none of the mission agencies I approached were working in Jakarta. Nor were any of them following a tentmaking approach to ministry. Frustrated, I decided to suspend my seminary studies for a year, go to

Indonesia to see for myself what was happening there, then to return to the U.S. and complete my studies. After that I would return to Indonesia full-time.

One Sunday, as I stood in the church lobby, my mission pastor came up and asked, "How are your preparations for ministry in Indonesia coming along, Matt?"

Certainly, if God wanted me to leave for Indonesia sooner and without being a part of a mission agency, He would need to bring my church on board. So I looked straight at my pastor and poured out my frustration over all the closed doors.

"Matt," the pastor said, "perhaps God has a different plan for you. Maybe you should just go."

I could hardly believe what I was hearing! One by one, God was removing each obstacle that stood in the way of my departure.

Even so, I'm afraid many people looked at me, listened to my plans, and shook their heads in disbelief. No wonder. I must have been the most hopeless missionary candidate ever. When my pastor did my commissioning service, he brought me up to platform and asked, "So, what have you done to prepare yourself to be a missionary?"

Well, let's see... I had no mission agency behind me. I knew next to nothing about Indonesia. All I could say was, "Well, I read a bunch of books."

***

People often asked, "How do you know God wants you to go to Indonesia?"

Half jokingly I would reply, "Because I don't like cold winters!"

Joking, maybe, yet it was true. I dreaded being cold. Every year as winter approached, I hoped someone would give me an electric blanket. As my family celebrated what would be our last Christmas together for a long while, my mother handed me a large, bulky present. I tore the wrapping paper off. Yes! I finally got my long-awaited electric blanket. But then reality sunk in: I was going to be a missionary. I had to be prepared to suffer. So I put the blanket in the back of my closet. I didn't even remove it from the package.

One frigid winter day in early February, I was telling my friend about the electric blanket and how, after wanting it for so many long winters, I wouldn't use it. "Because I want to train myself for the mission field," I said.

My friend smirked. "You're going to the tropics, aren't you? You should turn that electric blanket on high and sleep with your winter jacket on. Then you'll really be preparing yourself for life in Indonesia."

That was all the convincing I needed. I pulled out the blanket and used it the rest of that winter.

In April 1990, with $1,000 in my pocket and a one way plane ticket, I left for Indonesia.

CHAPTER 2

Where to Plant?

For hours, I had seen nothing from the airplane window except cloud-streaked blue sky. But now that sky blue seemed to melt into the azure sea below. I pressed my forehead against the window and stared down at the coral islands that dotted the sea. Indonesia! After so many years of preparation, I could actually see it. At long last, I would begin the ministry for which the Lord had been preparing me.

As the plane began its descent into Jakarta, the Dutch man next to me asked why I was coming to Indonesia.

"I quit my job," I told him. "I'm moving here."

"Why?" he exclaimed. "I cannot think of any reason you would want to move here!"

His response so startled me that doubts crept into my mind. What *was* I doing? Could I have been wrong about the Lord's leading?

Of Indonesia's 230 million people, nearly 90 percent are Muslim. The strong and vibrant Indonesian church has been raised up by the Lord to reach the country with the gospel.

God, in His sovereignty, established a Christian people group on each of the major islands. Bataks on Sumatra, Javanese on Java, Dayaks on Kalimantan, Minahasa on Sulawesi. Yet also on all of these islands are large and seldomly evangelized Muslim people groups. What could I do in such a place? A 25-year-old with no extraordinary gifts, virtually no experience, and no special status? How could I possibly hope to engage the church to reach out to those Muslim groups? Short answer: not much.

I arrived in Indonesia in the middle of a month of fasting, a time when family and friends fast and eat together, and spend most of their time in each other's company. I had neither family nor friends in the country, which gave me a lot of time to wait and watch and reflect. Still, the night I arrived, an Indonesian fellow took me to church with him for a small evening service of about 100 believers. I understood next to nothing of what was said during the two-hour service. Even so, the local Christians impressed me deeply. Two days later, I went to the main service. More than 400 people crammed in to the rented building to worship God. I still remember the pastor's sermon: It took God forty days to get His people out of Egypt, but it took Him forty years to get Egypt out of them.

My Indonesian contacts were scarce and not too helpful, so I sought out people who were already at work among Muslims in the capital city of Jakarta. I wanted to find out what was going on and how I might get involved in it. I knocked on one particular door that was opened by Jeff Gulleson, a missionary who had been in the country twenty-five years. He invited me to sit with him in the living room of his rented house. Jeff, who had seen many people come and go on the mission field, asked, "So, how are you going to reach the Muslims of Indonesia?"

The question caught me off guard. How? To be honest, I hadn't given that much thought. So far, I'd had all I could do to simply follow my call and get to Indonesia. The *do* didn't leave much energy to invest in the *how*. I started to talk about the things I was getting involved in, such as helping a youth group at an Indonesian church.

"But how are you going to reach millions of Muslims by working with a church youth group?" Jeff interrupted. He did believe in getting right to the heart of the matter.

I had uprooted myself from a successful career. I had moved half way around the world. Yet I had never really thought things through! What was the matter with me? That certainly was not following good engineering practices. Before I ever started, I should have put together a plan along with a way to implement it.

For an uncomfortable while, Jeff and I sat in silence. Fortunately, he provided me with a way out. "Look, next week we are meeting to form the first Indonesian mission agency to work exclusively with Muslims. Why don't you come along and see what's going on?"

At that meeting, I got to know leaders of an Indonesian denomination who wanted to launch an outreach to Muslims beginning with the *Sundanese* people. The leaders saw the people's spiritual need, but they didn't know how to go about doing the work. Yet they were committed to allowing the local mission agency to work freely among the various denominations of the country so that they could fully connect with *all* God's people in the country.

"So," the leaders asked, "how about it? Will you help us?"

Sundanese? Who were they? I had no idea.

I knew that Java—an island about the size of the state of Illinois—has around 60 percent of Indonesia's population. (That's like half the population of the U.S. crowded into the state of Illinois!) The Javanese, from the central-eastern part of the island, are the largest people group in the country. They

have also experienced the largest turning to Christ in the history of Muslim missions. In the past 120 or 130 years, approximately twelve million Javanese have become Christians.

I knew all that. What I didn't know until Jeff explained it to me was that the Sundanese are the second largest people group in the country. They live in one-third of the same island. Being Sundanese is sort of like being the less talented younger brother. Although the two groups share the island of Java, the Javanese are the dominant culture. For instance, because of the Javanese possess a strong work ethic, they go to the lands of the Sunda, and soon they take many of the good the jobs. Here's another difference: Of the 35 million Sundanese people, few had come to faith. A people extremely resistant to the gospel, they have been called the world's largest unreached people group. But at the time, I didn't know any of this.

"Well?" he pressed. "Will you help us?"

Other than helping with the youth group, I had nothing going on. So I agreed.

Jakarta's 13 million people represent a major mixture of all the people groups in Indonesia. About one million are Christians. Yet if you get in your car and drive for an hour, you will find yourself in the midst of the world's largest unreached people group. It's not as if the Sundanese are some jungle group, where it might take days and days to chop your way through to reach them. You don't need a visa. You don't need travel permission. Just get in the car and drive. How could such a thing be? So many Christians across the street from so many who have never heard!

The more I learned about the Sundanese, the more eager I became to begin planning. On October 15 through 18, 1990, we held a planning retreat to establish the goals of the mission and to lay out a plan for getting started. It drew upon the resources of many groups already working among the Sundanese people. All together, we represented some 200 years of Indonesian ministry, and 25 years of Sundanese ministry. That's significant. All that expertise is what helped us establish a firm foundation for the new mission. And with 35 million Sundanese unreached, what amazing potential!

There are many reasons for the Sundanese people's resistance to the gospel. A main reason is their more rigid approach to Islam, which means a total intolerance of family members who change religions. This, of course, creates problems for missionaries bringing the gospel. Unlike Javanese who are Javanese first and Muslim second, Sundanese are Muslim first and foremost. Because Indonesians have much greater freedom to minister than Westerners do, a strategy of equipping and sending Indonesian church planters made great sense. Even so, if we hoped to plant churches capable of surviving in the Sundanese culture, we would need to find a new way of thinking.

One thing that really excited us was the possibility that the new mission could become a model for other Indonesian missions. From the Indonesian point of view, what we put together was truly revolutionary in that it focused on an unreached Muslim people group. Until then, Indonesian missions were either general in focus, encompassing many ethnic groups, or else they focused on specific animist tribes. This new approach could help the Indonesian church develop a whole new vision to spread the gospel to ethnic groups who had no Christian witness among their own people. Considering that approximately half the country's 230 million people are from ethnic groups without any Christian witness, it was a hugely significant advance. And with all the trouble foreign missionaries were having obtaining visas to come to Indonesia, the only way those closed ethnic groups would ever hear the gospel would be from Indonesians.

God was at work. We all knew it. And looking back on the timing of various contacts, and the way everyone came together, it could only have happened by God's design. The potential for the mission was only as great as God's involvement in it. That's always true, of course, but it was especially so with Sundanese Muslims. Unless God opened the doors, prepared the hearts, and led His people, it couldn't happen.

My mom often says she needs to get her ducks in a row before she can do something. I, on the other hand, had no ducks at all. Sometimes it's best not to know what is going to happen. If I had done a better job of thinking things through, I might never have obeyed God and gone to Indonesia. Had I known then what I know now about how much work it takes to launch such an agency, I probably never would have agreed to it. When it comes to following God, there is something to be said for a sort of naivety. Like Abraham, we are forced to walk by faith. To move forward step by step, even when we have no idea what lies ahead. That's exactly what we did. It was the only way.

As we met to discuss the new mission agency, I got to know many of the denominational leaders. They had a deep love for the Lord and a true burden to reach the Muslims in their country. I also began to learn about some of the cultural barriers that hindered the church's work among Muslims. One was the mutual prejudice between the Chinese and Muslim communities. The Chinese, who have lived in Indonesia for several generations, often view the Muslims as troublemakers who threatened to expel them from what had become their country. In 1997, Chinese stores were targeted in Jakarta. The riots forced many Chinese to flee the country and never return. On the other hand, the Muslims feel oppressed by the uncircumcised, pork eating, economically advantaged Chinese. This unfortunate dynamic hinders interaction between the communities. Nor is the church immune to the prejudices. Indonesia has many strong Chinese churches, but the prejudice between these communities impedes the churches from reaching out to the Muslims.

Over the years, I have worked with many ethnic Chinese brothers and sisters who deeply love the Lord and truly wanted to introduce Christ to the Muslims. Our mission agency provided them with another way to do so. In one of our first meetings, a businessman stated, "I want to share the gospel with Muslims, but because I am Chinese they will not allow me to get near them. But by serving on the board of directors for this mission, I can have a part in evangelizing the Sundanese."

And so the Sundanese Christian Fellowship (SCF) was launched. Its commitment was to evangelize the Sundanese people and plant contextual house churches among those who believe. Contextual because if we ever hoped to communicate the gospel to them, we must be able to speak to their worldview: who they are, their history, their beliefs. If we don't understand culture, we don't understand anything.

In my March 1991 prayer letter I wrote: "For the first time since I arrived in Indonesia, I feel as though I have turned the corner in respect to the work here. I am taking much more serious my call to service in West Java. I am certain that this change has been the direct result of the prayers of the saints. Such a change could not have taken place unless someone has been weeping before God for me."

It was true. Four years earlier, when I drove through West Java, it disturbed me that the Sundanese people had no witness among them. Even so, I felt an overwhelming helplessness. I had no idea what I could do to help. After I returned to the States, the question continued to burn inside me: "How can I help them? How?" I had no answers. All I knew was that it must be done!

Thanks to groups like the Sundanese Christian Fellowship, that question no longer haunts me. It no longer plunges me into feelings of helplessness. Instead, I am flooded by the sheer enormity of the task.

It is not right that so many people who long to hear don't have the opportunity.

The walls of Satan's kingdom had already begun to crumble. The power of God was already crushing Satan's strongholds in West Java. My vision had never been greater. God had spoken! More importantly, I listened.

CHAPTER 3

A Struggling Sprout

One morning, I went out to a village to see an especially majestic waterfall. On the way back, no minivan was heading into the city, so I started to walk. Another guy, a Sundanese school teacher, was also going to the city, so we started to walk together. I had learned enough of the language to share the gospel, so I prayed, "Here's my opportunity." As I walked, I began to tell him about the gospel and how he could have eternal life. I was flabbergasted at his response, which was no response at all. I got more reaction from the rocks on the side of the road than I did from that guy! The gospel simply was not relating to where he was. No connection at all.

That was my first experience of sharing the gospel with a Sundanese. Wonderful people. Very friendly and willing to listen. But how could I make the gospel penetrate? How could I make it relate to their needs? To their lives?

Putting the concept for a local mission agency down on paper was the easy part. Figuring out how to actually recruit and send Indonesians to do Sundanese church planting was a whole different story.

At the beginning of the 16th century, the Hindu kingdom of Pajajaran controlled West Java. But in 1527, the Muslim Javanese kingdom of Demak sent Muslim missionaries to the area. They succeeded in defeating the Hindu kingdom. These Muslim preachers communicated the teachings of Islam in culturally relevant ways to which the Sundanese people could easily relate. The Sundanese temperament was ideally suited for assimilating new teachings, and the Islam brought to West Java fit right into the their worldview.

When Dutch traders came in 1596, they brought hope that at last the gospel would be preached to the Sundanese. But that's not what happened. The Dutch East Indies Company[1] placed a greater emphasis on business and profit than on establishing Christ's kingdom among the Sundanese. In fact, in order to keep the peace, they actively hindered the work of evangelism. The traders came as colonizers that were difficult to approach, and that created a division between the Europeans and the Sundanese. Islam became a rallying point against the white man from foreign lands. Serious mission activity was not permitted until the middle of the 19th century. Although few in number, early missionaries labored faithfully against tremendous odds. Even so, they largely failed because they did not pay attention to the Sundanese culture. So the Sundanese people came to view the gospel as European. They were convinced that anyone who became a Christian would have to stop being Sundanese. Christian converts would become like the Europeans.

---

[1] In Dutch, *Vereenigde Oost-Indische Compagnie* (VOC) was established in 1602 and granted a monopoly trade with the Netherland's eastern colonial entities. The VOC held this monopoly until it went bankrupt in 1796.

Over the centuries, many different beliefs and religions have been brought to the shores of West Java. Of them all, Islam has the most adherents. One out of every six Indonesians is Sundanese, and almost all of them are Muslim. Less than one-tenth of one percent are Christians.

The Sundanese are extremely religious. From their large cities to outlying villages, they actively build mosques and Islamic prayer rooms. But Sundanese Islam is a mixture of animism, Buddhism, Hinduism, and Islamic mysticism. Islam, a relative late-comer, provided another layer to the previous belief system foundation. The resulting folk Islam is evident in the Sundanese life-cycle rituals. They embrace all of life's major events, starting from before birth—cutting the umbilical cord, taking first steps, circumcision, marriage, burial—and they continue until 1,000 days after death. These rituals form a circle in which the two ends of a life meet together again. By following in the footsteps of their ancestors, the rituals allow the Sundanese people to reach their life's destination. But these rituals also serve to acknowledge and pacify the unseen spirits surrounding the Sundanese.

I once interviewed the head of the Islamic center outside Jakarta, asking him about Islam. After I turned off my tape recorder, he said, "Have you seen the tigers?" Puzzled, I asked what he meant. "Tiger spirits. I saw them when I was driving home one day, down a mountain pass. All these tigers in the road."

Whether the story is true or simply a myth, the Sundanese believe that Prabu Siliwangi, the leader of the Hindu Sundanese kingdom, faced the advancing Muslim armies of Cirebon and Banten. As his forces gave up ground to the Muslim army, Prabu Siliwangi and his troops receded into the jungles surrounding Mount Salak. Outnumbered and surrounded, Prabu Siliwangi's soldiers were turned into tigers while Prabu Siliwangi himself *ngahyang*, that is disappeared. Although the Sundanese tell many variations of this story, the legend is something known to by all of them. As the man at the Islamic center related it to me, many still today claim seeing the spirits of tigers roaming around West Java and Banten. To pay homage to the spirit of Prabu Siliwangi, many have pictures of tigers in their homes or erected statues of tigers in public spaces. Even though they are Islamic, there is still a core of belief in the spirit world. That belief along with life-cycle rituals reach down to that core. This is all part of the context.

The Sundanese worldview includes a pantheon of spirits that watch over the people day and night. Haunted by spirits from on top of trees or behind graves, in times of trouble the people turn to the burial places of important ancestors. The keeper of the grave makes intercession with the spirits of "holy ones," on behalf of a person in need, asking for blessings or help. People go to the graves on Thursday nights and offer goat meat, flowers or different kinds of food sacrifices in order to gain favor and get help with their problems. Sundanese people believe that these intercessors have mystical powers that allow them to do miracles, or heal illness, or even disappear. Once I was talking to a Muslim shaman, and he said, "Excuse me if I disappear while I'm talking to you. It happens sometimes. I'm really still here but you just can't see me." Even Muslim leaders address the spirit world around them.

It's difficult for Westerners, who have no similar ties, to understand the importance of these life-cycle rituals. Passed down from generation to generation, they have become rooted in the very being of the Sundanese people, and are integrated into their religion. Ethnicity, culture, and Islam have fused together so tightly that the people see becoming a Christian as deserting their identity. Converts often face challenges, alienation, and even persecution. This cultural isolation is enough to keep most people in line. One new almost-believer was so very close to coming to Christ. Then a neighbor commented, "Oh, so you are going to become a Christian." Just that one sentence. It was enough to make her stop all contact.

The Sundanese family also presents challenges to evangelism and discipleship. A Sundanese wedding ceremony is a beautiful event that involves the entire community in much tradition. But half of all marriages end in divorce. The Sundanese have a saying: *"Kawin ayeuna, esuk papagatan,"* which means: "Today we marry, tomorrow we divorce." As a matter of fact, they view divorce and remarriage as a sign of desirability. For them, it is more embarrassing to never marry than to be married for a single night and then divorced. One lady told me, "I have only married for the eighth time." Evidently, she expects more marriages to come! After all, if eight men wanted to marry her, who could doubt that she was desirable?

Another time I met a man out in the village who told me he had been married 22 times. "The shortest lasted two nights," he said.

Such rampant divorce and remarriage plays havoc on the Sundanese community. Children are often raised by a grandmother because their mother's new husband doesn't want to care for someone else's offspring.

This also caused problems when we discipled new Christians. Siddik and his wife were some of the first people won to the Lord by Sundanese Christian Fellowship workers.

Siddik was the wife's eighth husband and she was his twelfth wife. One night, ex-husband number seven came to Siddik's house drunk, demanding to borrow money from his ex-wife. Siddik awoke and heard what was going on. His jealously flared, and he stormed out of the house. That night he slept at the house of ex-wife number ten's home. How can we handle such a situation? How can we help these two to grow to be more like Christ? This was not part of the seminary pastoral counseling curriculum!

By God's grace, I met a man who helped guide me through this process. He and his wife had been working among the Sundanese since 1969. They took me under their wings and taught me how to be a missionary. At least once a month, I rode three hours to Bandung on a crowded train, often sitting on the floor all the way, just to be with them. We would spend several days discussing the work among the Sundanese while drinking ice tea and eating cake.

That family helped me with issues relating to Sundanese culture as well as with situations that arose within the SCF ministry team. One important thing he helped me understand was the need of a cultural approach. It's not so much Islam that's keeping Sundanese from the gospel, it's the lack of Sundanese-ness in the gospel. The good news of Jesus Christ is viewed as a Western thing.

They also showed me how to shepherd new believers. Many of the ones who did come to faith were returning to Islam because they were not being shepherded. This is so vital. They have a whole system at work, trying to pull them back. Islam, Islam, Islam. Everything is Islam. Except for two hours a week when they attend a church service. All society, every conversation, all dealings with the government. So how does a new believer keep faith alive? Only through stronger shepherding networks.

For much of the first four years, the Sundanese Christian Fellowship struggled just to survive. The Indonesian denomination that gave birth to SCF provided us with our first leader. We recruited our first worker and sent him to a six month training course in a Sundanese ministry run by the man in Bandung who so effectively mentored me. Then at the end of the training, that first worker resigned. Launching a pioneering work proved to be a difficult undertaking!

Our problems were made all the more difficult by our Indonesian leader's health challenges, the result of a car crash several months before he joined us. Almost every day, he battled painful migraines and paralysis down his left side. We took him to several doctors, but they found nothing wrong with him. Yet every day he endured terrible pain. Because of the debilitating medical problem, he functioned at a low capacity. And as anyone who has started a business or ministry knows, a start-up requires extra capacity, not lower.

"If I were to sum up my experience since I arrived in one word, that word would be stress." That's what I wrote in my September 1991 prayer letter. It wasn't only me, either. A good friend told me that so many workers focused on ministry to Muslims, both Indonesian and foreign, drop out because the ministry is so stressful.

Because of the overwhelming spiritual darkness of this area, everyone who labors in West Java feels the pressure. That's why I quickly came to see prayer as so very important. Only through prayer could any of us hope to persevere. Only through prayer would light shine in the land.

In the tropics, when it rains it pours. The same can be said of the stressful season in West Java. Satan gets credit for those well-rounded attacks. He hit with everything at once. But praise God, our Protector and Provider. He had already bound up the strongman and robbed him of his treasures. My prayer was that the people would be able to cling firmly to Him and His truth.

The reality of God's promises concerning this work did not make me immune from having doubts or struggles. There was a season when I wrestled before the Lord. *What am I doing here?* I wondered. *Perhaps I should go back to America and my career as a computer engineer.*

But the Lord interrupted my doubts and reminded me of my calling. He was the one who had called me to Indonesia. He was the one who placed me with the Sundanese people. My job was to hold firm to that calling. In His mercy, God opened up a door for me to go to the U.S. for a month-long furlough.

I had no idea how much I needed that time at home. For months I had been struggling to grasp hold of patience and joy. I was so overwhelmed that things had spun way out of perspective. How thankful I am that God saw my needs even when I could not.

David wrote in Psalm 30: "I called to you for help and you healed me." But I didn't even call, because I didn't realize how in need of healing I was. Looking back, I see that God sent me home to heal me. As my friends ministered to me with patience and love, I fell on God, pleading for mercy. He heard me, and He answered.

I returned to Indonesia recharged, and with a whole new perspective.

After more than a year, the difficult decision was made to replace the leader of SCF. Even though there was no one on the horizon to take his place. Once again our fledging outreach rested completely in the hands of God. But then, what better place could it be?

CHAPTER 4

The Cost of Setting Root

Domu entered seminary in 1985 to pursue his Master of Divinity degree. His goal was to be a pastor. As his graduation approached, he told the chairman of his church's elder board about his desire. The elder pointed Domu to one of the synod's churches on the island of Mentawai, off the coast of West Sumatra. "Here is where you should go," he said. "This church recently collapsed. It badly needs new leadership. You could be the man God uses to bring the congregation back to life."

Domu's church was affiliated with the Batak Christian Protestant Church (HKBP)[1], a denomination with a truly amazing history. Not many missionaries attempted to work among the Batak people. Several who did were subsequently killed. Nommensen, a German missionary, continued in the pursuit of bringing the gospel to the Bataks. When he came to the Silindung valley overlooking the Batak heartland Nommensen prayed, "Alive or dead, let me live in the midst of this people to spread the word and kingdom." And the people

---

[1] In Indonesia, the name of the denomination is *Huria Kristen Batak Protestan*

did try to poison him. They also tried to eat him. One time they held a party where he was to be the main dish! God dispersed the party by sending a bolt of lightning. Nommensen started a whole movement among the animistic people, and hundreds of thousands of Bataks came to Christ. But since the end of World

War II, the denomination had embraced liberal theology, and was in decline. Even so, Domu eagerly accepted the challenge of pastoring one of their churches. But during his six-month orientation, synod leaders saw that Domu's beliefs really were evangelical. That didn't sit at all well with the synod's liberal leadership, so they released him.

Needless to say, Domu was dejected by this unexpected turn of events. One day he was preparing for a challenging new ministry, and the next he found himself cast adrift with no ministry at all. He contacted Jeff Gulleson, who had been one of his seminary instructors. Jeff opened his house to Domu, and the two of them discussed Domu's future.

"I don't know what to do," Domu told him. "I am all set to depart with my wife and three children, but I have no place to go. Nowhere to serve the Lord."

"Well, let me tell you about a new outreach that was just started," Jeff said. "The goal is to reach the 35 million Sundanese Muslims. Their leader is too ill to work, so they need to replace him. You would really be a tremendous blessing to the group."

Domu shook his head. "Honestly I don't find that appealing. I see myself more as a seminary instructor or a pastor. I really enjoy pastoral counseling." Domu paused for a moment, then he quickly added, "Anyway, I don't know a thing about missions. I studied Biblical Theology. I never thought of the mission courses as interesting."

Jeff leaned forward and looked Domu in the eye. "The people in the Batak Protestant Christian Church have heard the gospel hundreds, perhaps thousands of times. Yet there are more than 35 million Sundanese, and very few of them believe in Christ. From birth until death, they have not heard the gospel even once. Is that fair?"

Jeff's words hit Domu like a whip. Domu left the house promising to discuss the matter with his wife and to bring it before the Lord in prayer.

That night Domu tossed and turned on his bed. *From birth until death, they have not heard the gospel even once. Is that fair?* Over and over, Jeff's words rang in his ears. *Is that fair? Is that fair?*

If he were to decide to join SCF, Domu worried how well the new organization would be able to provide for this wife and three young children. After all, the ministry was only a year old. Every morning, in their family devotions, he and his wife and children brought the matter before the Lord. One morning they read from Matthew 6:25-33:

> *"Therefore I tell you, do not worry about your life, what you will eat or drink; or about your body, what you will wear. Is not life more than food, and the body more than clothes? Look at the birds of the air; they do not sow or reap or store away in barns, and yet your heavenly Father feeds them. Are you not much more valuable than they? Can any one of you by worrying add a single hour to your life? And why do you worry about clothes? See how the flowers of the field grow. They do not labor or spin. Yet I tell you that not even Solomon in all his splendor was dressed like one of these. If that is how God clothes the grass of the field, which is here today and tomorrow is thrown into the fire, will he not much more clothe you—you of little faith? So do not worry, saying, 'What shall we eat?' or 'What shall we drink?' or 'What shall we wear?' For the pagans run after all these things, and your heavenly Father knows that you need them. But seek first his kingdom and his righteousness, and all these things will be given to you as well."*

Domu's first child would be entering elementary school, and the second one would be in kindergarten. The monthly stipend from SCF would not be enough to cover the school fees. Domu knew they could not ask for additional funds from SCF. The mission was new, and it barely had enough money to cover its monthly expenses. "I have often preached from this passage,"

Domu told his wife. "But today the Lord is saying to me, 'This Word is not just for other people, but for you as well.'"

It is easy to instruct others in God's Word, but difficult to instruct ourselves.

But that day, Domu felt the Lord standing before him, saying, "This Word is for you."

Both Domu and his wife began to weep. "Lord, this is my wife, these are my children," Domu prayed. "You know that I am filled with worry. This morning I have heard You say that we do not need to worry. We want to go wherever You call us, and we do not care what happens to us. Our only prayer is that Your will be done."

Thus began a new chapter for SCF. Domu moved his family to the greater Jakarta metropolitan area. We opened an office in the back of my rented house and dove into the work with a new enthusiasm. Enthusiasm, however, that was met with confusion. We still did not really know what we should be doing. We still had no model to follow. Domu sought direction from the board, but they too had little to offer.

Looking back on that time, Domu said, "Those early years were full of struggle where I found myself often crying out to the Lord, 'What should I work on?' I had no direction from the leadership because I only met with them once a month at a prayer meeting. I was so frustrated that I began to think about leaving this ministry. But the Lord gave me a confirmation that strengthened me. His clear calling for my family is the only reason we remained until now."

One great difficulty was that we had no staff. We began prayer meetings in three cities to pray specifically for the

Sundanese, and some new recruits did begin to appear. But because we were not adept at running the ministry, they left one by one. All except one. SCF consisted of Domu and myself, one church planter, and eight board members. Week after week, Domu and I met with that single church planter, Sutrisno. Together we meditated on God's Word, prayed, and discussed the ministry. But even as we met, the question nagged at the back of our minds: Would SCF even survive? There were some faithful Indonesian supporters, but at the beginning of some months we didn't even have enough funds to cover salaries. And yet, by the end of the month, God always provided what was lacking.

"Everything was done by faith," Domu recalls. "We learned a lot from our difficulties and failures. My fellowship and sharing with Matt helped strengthen me."

Throughout this transition Domu's wife, Tati, carried the tremendous burden of learning how to care for her family while the men were away. Besides taking care of the household, she had long days of separation as Domu and I poured ourselves into developing the ministry. Since I was still single, I had no idea how much time and work a family needs.

"Sometimes Matt and I would get carried away discussing and planning the ministry and I would come home late at night," Domu says. "My wife was frustrated because she had three small children at home and I was not around to help much. But the Lord is good. He provided for the needs of my children."

As Domu and I worked hard, Tati held the home together. She also took advantage of any opportunity to meet Sundanese women and minister to them. This period was very difficult for her, but she slowly began to understand. "I also had to do my part to build up SCF," Tati says of that time.

Without Tati's support ,SCF would not have gone forward. Even when she was sick, or alone at home with the problems of raising the children, she continued to stand alongside her husband in his ministry. She got involved with other women in community activities, and God used that to shape her for her own future ministry of teaching the younger wives how to serve alongside their husbands. No one knows like one who has been there.

As Domu's family worked to adjust to the new ministry, I faced struggles of my own. As a self-support tentmaking missionary, I only had money when I worked. Yet the ministry was growing, and Domu and I were getting busier and busier. I didn't have much time for outside work. But finally, with the money running out, I needed to get another job. I got a government contract that paid quite well. The only problem was that the paper work got stuck in the system, and although I was working, I was not getting paid.

"I lift up my eyes to you, to you whose throne is in heaven. As the eyes of slaves look to the hand of their master, as the eyes of a maid look to the hand of her mistress, so our eyes look to the Lord our God, till he shows us his mercy." (Psalm 123:1-2)

The Psalmist wrote it, but I clung to it. Tightly. For six months. I worked, but I received no income. Still, God provided. Not all I wanted. But just enough to make ends meet.

Difficult times are lesson times. God used that lean, frustrating time to remind me that everything I enjoy comes from His hand. It's easy to forget that every day of our lives is completely dependent on God. Hard time teach us to fix our eyes on Him so we can watch His goodness flow. A heady lesson indeed.

Not that it's easy. It most certainly is not! Twice I found myself with absolutely no money other than the change in my pocket. But time and again the Lord provided—not only for me, but for all the church planters.

And blessing on top of blessings, it was during this period that I met Nina, a young lady at church. An Indonesian, she had spent five years in America studying music and accounting. As we got to know each other, I could not help but recognize her heart for the Lord and her desire to serve Him. Nina's prayer was that the Lord would give her a husband with whom she could serve the Lord. We did talk about the possibility of pursuing a relationship, but I was terrified of marriage. What really frightened me was that marriage is so... so... *permanent.* Nothing in my entire life had ever been permanent. Even coming to Indonesia was not an irreversible decision. But that wasn't all. I was also afraid I would end up being controlled by her family. It wasn't an empty fear, either. In Indonesia, many parents still control the lives of their adult children. But after running my own life so long, that was the absolute last thing I wanted. So I did the only thing that made sense to me; I ran away. I completely ignored Nina. It was the end for us. Well, for several months, anyway.

In January 1994, I contracted my first bout of typhoid. I had no idea what it was, so I suffered at home for many days before I finally going to the hospital. They kept me there for nearly a week. When I called my mom to tell her about my condition, she became hysterical. She had no idea what typhoid was, but since I'd spent a week in the hospital, she figured it must be serious. "Look it up before you freak out," I told her. She did, and the next day she called me back, much more out of control. A little information... how dangerous it can be!

During my hospital stay, Nina came to minister to me. She passed by the hospital on her way to and from work, so every day she stopped in to talk. That's how we got to know one another. As she cut mangos for me, we talked about my fear of parental control. Day after day she came, and day after day we talked. Nine months later, we married.

The challenges Domu and I went through between 1992 and 1994—in our own lives as well as in the ministry—forged more than just a relationship between us. We grew to be true brothers. As we developed SCF's ministry, we became more and more involved in one another's families. We spent many nights on the road mobilizing Indonesian churches by showing them the needs of the Sundanese Muslims. The ministry distributed more than 100,000 tracts in the Sundanese language. Even so, all our efforts were like pouring salt in the ocean. People put so much trust and confidence in us, yet we had little to show for it.

We weren't the only ones to struggle with discouragement. Many other workers believed that things would happen quickly. But that was not to be in our ministry among Sundanese Muslims. That requires four or five years of planting seeds, then nurturing them along, before lasting fruit appears.

CHAPTER 5

A Garden Plant

"Sundanese Christian Fellowship is looking for men and women who are called to share God's love with the people in West Java."

When that announcement crackled over the radio, Satrio perked up. The words echoed in his heart. Could God be calling him?

Over the next three months, Satrio and his wife Lina spent much time in prayer, seeking the Lord's guidance. One day, kneeling together in a prayer garden outside their city, they prayed, "You must be the one to send us, Lord. We do not want to go out of our own fleshly desires."

At the time, Satrio was pasturing a church in Central Java, home to the tremendous movement of the Lord among Muslims. Beginning back in 1860, the Javanese began to steadily embrace Christianity, and that growth continues to this day. When Satrio was growing up, his family was the first in his village to believe in Christ. In high school, his Muslim classmates teased him about his faith and generally made life difficult for him. But ask him about today, and he will happily report, "Forty percent of my village is Christian! In fact, many of the ones who teased me in high school have entered the ministry and are pastoring churches!"

But Satrio and Lina hoped to serve God in a different place, somewhere where few people knew Christ. They decided to join SCF. Satrio wrote out his letter of application, then he sealed the envelope. "Lina," he said, "if we work as church planters, we must be prepared to suffer all kinds of difficulties – not enough money, poor schooling for our children, all kind of trials. We must be willing to live a simple life."

"I'm willing," Lina replied.

A great sense of peace filled their hearts and enveloped them. With new enthusiasm, Satrio began the course.

Without a doubt, God was calling Satrio and Lina, and others like them, into His harvest field. Domu and I had committed ourselves to obeying the Lord's command in Matthew 9:37-38: *"The harvest is plentiful but the workers are few. Ask the Lord of the harvest, therefore, to send out workers into his harvest field."* As we and others around the world prayed, God worked in hearts, calling people to West Java. But it was one thing to recruit and quite another to find ways to present the gospel to the Sundanese Muslims. The cross-cultural Indonesian church planters needed to understand how to enter new cultures and integrate with new communities. They needed to learn to effectively proclaim the gospel in an unfamiliar place. Of course, many missionaries around the world have this same difficulty. But with so many people groups in Indonesia, so many personalities and religious cultures, it was a particular challenge.

"As soon as we arrived in West Java, we went from house to house sharing the gospel," Satrio recalled. "But it wasn't as easy as we thought it would be."

Lina smiled and shook her head at the memory. "We moved into an undeveloped community and were the only Christians in that area. Most of the people there had little education and couldn't even speak the national language, and we hadn't yet learned the Sundanese dialect. The people spat on us because they considered Christians to be *najis*[1]. We couldn't understand what was happening. We asked the Lord, 'Why do they hate us?'"

The couple rented a house on the edge of the city. After four frustrating months, a teenager came to faith. But over the next year and a half, Lina and Satrio faced various sorts of intimidation because of that young man's decision to follow Christ. "Nearly every night, people would throw rocks at our house," Satrio said. "At two a.m., they smashed in my daughter's bedroom window. From then on, she would shake in fear at the sound of stones hitting our house. Other times, people cut the cables that brought electricity to our house. This didn't go on for only a day or a week. It continued for a year and a half!"

Satrio began to wonder, "Were we really called to this place?" And who could blame him? All those problems because one single person believed in Christ. What would

---

[1] Indonesian meaning unclean or impure. Islam, like Judaism, has a strict code of laws which determines the purity or impurity of something. Christians are considered impure for several reasons. Muslims accuse them of worshipping three gods (Father, Son, and Mary), eating unclean food such as pork, and not being circumcised in Indonesia.

happen when others came to faith? "But my wife never wavered in her calling," Satrio says. "She strengthened me during this time."

The situation in their neighborhood was growing worse by the day. After church one week, the young man who had come to Christ warned Satrio and Lina, "Don't go home. My family stirred up the neighborhood and they are all waiting for you. They are really angry because I believe in Jesus."

Satrio was so shocked he couldn't utter a single word in response. But then Lina could. "Regardless of the situation, I'm going home!" she announced. "I am not afraid!"

Heartened by his wife's courage, Satrio helped her and their daughter onto the motorbike for the trip home. As they approached the house, they saw a group of men gathered at the entrance of the five-foot-wide path that led from the street to their house. "We knew the risk we were facing," Satrio says of that day. "There was a great possibility we would be beaten, perhaps even killed. We say we are ready to die for Christ, but when we saw that mob, it crushed our courage."

Satrio asked the men to move so he could pass by, but they did not. So Satrio gave his motorbike a burst of gas and roared directly toward them. The men barely managed to jump out of the way.

Satrio and Lina made it safely into their house. As soon as they got inside, they knelt down and prayed for the Lord's protection. And He answered them. The crowd gave up and went home.

Soon afterwards, a financial crisis hit Indonesia, and the country's currency collapsed. Many families suffered severe economic hardship. SCF took the disaster as an opportunity to minister to Muslim communities in practical ways. Church planters approached the leaders of the villages and worked with them to bring in discounted food for the people most affected by the rising prices. In one village, the Muslim leader refused the help because it came from Christians. But after several months with no assistance from Muslims, the villagers turned on their leader. Finally, he came to SCF to apologize and ask if assistance was still available. It most certainly was.

That economic crisis drew a stark contrast between the love exhibited by Christians and the inaction of Muslim groups toward the needy. My personal research shows that this is the biggest single human factor that brings a Muslim to faith: they experience love from Christians. Jesus Himself instructed His followers to help others because "whatever you did for one of the least of these brothers and sisters of mine, you did for me" (Matthew 25:40). Muslims, on the other hand, view those who are poor, sick, or uneducated as cursed by God. They believe no one can change the fate God preordained for such people.

When Satrio and Lina organized the distribution of food staples in their community, the people were amazed. After all the ill-treatment that had been done to this family, how could it be that they responded with such kindness? Since that day, there has been no more terror against Satrio's family.

It was not easy to find "called" staff with the gifts for Muslim church planting. Neither was it easy to retain the ones who came. Domu and I learned a lot about how to structure the ministry so that church planters would have the proper shepherding and supervision they needed. It's not like ministry in a church. These church planters lived in remote areas, often with no other Christians nearby. If they were to serve successfully in such difficult places, they needed special attention.

Suri smiled as she tore open the letter from her boyfriend, Yudi. He had been working with SCF for a year, and she was looking forward to the time when they would be together. She unfolded the letter and read: "The ministry here is so different from church work. We are pioneering a ministry starting from zero. I want you to know that if you join me here as my wife, I will not be able to guarantee anything for you. We are completely dependent upon the Lord's provision." Suri's smile didn't falter. She wasn't discouraged by Yudi's words. The Lord would also use her in the ministry. Of that she was confident.

Two days after their wedding, Suri moved to West Java with Yudi. He showed her the SCF office. That's when her smile faded. The office was in a small, simple rented house—and was also to be their new home. "To save SCF money," Yudi explained. For the first time, doubts flooded over Suri.

As the stress of living as a newlywed in a cross-cultural situation without a place of their own wore on her, her doubts grew. Then one day Yudi told her that the mission didn't have enough money to pay salaries. "This month they will have to pay us in three installments," he said.

Who opens a ministry and recruits people if they don't have enough money to pay them? Suri thought. But she said nothing. She understood what was happening; her flesh was getting the best of her.

"This is the path we must follow," Yudi told her. "If we are faithful, God will honor our faithfulness."

Her husband's gentle patience reassured Suri. Holding fast to his words, her heart began to open to the ministry. But her struggle to trust God wasn't limited to finances. There was also the culture shock. Food, climate—most everything was the same as she was used to. Everything except the differences between Indonesian peoples. But those differences were significant. The Sudanese lack of discipline dismayed Suri. Whenever the people had money, it seemed that they would squander it. Many were in debt to several people at once. Yudi and Suri wanted to help their Sundanese friends by creating work for them, so they bought clothing and gave it to their friends to resell. The Sundanese agreed to pay Yudi and Suri back for the clothes and keep the profit for themselves. But that's not what happened. Their friends took the clothing and never returned. Yudi and Suri were left to cover the loss with their own meager funds. The whole situation in West Java plunged Suri into a deep depression.

Domu's wife, Tati, and my wife, Nina, started a Bible study for SCF women staff members. It was especially important to people like Suri. Through interaction with the other women, she learned to develop her own ministry, and also to support her husband's work. "Without that mentoring, I would never have remained in this ministry," Suri says. "It's so important to have co-workers who strengthen us when we are weak."

Suri knows this first-hand. "If we are faithful to the Lord, we don't need to worry about our physical needs because the Lord will take care of them," she says. "Right now I am discipling a woman who came to faith through my husband. Every week we meet together, and the growth in her life is amazing. Being a part of that gives me greater joy than if someone gave me a great deal of money."

SCF would not have made it this far without another component – the board of directors. Just as the new staff and their families needed mentoring and guidance, SCF needed people with experience who could develop the framework for future ministry. Domu and I could apply sweat and muscle to the task, but we needed competent oversight to guide us along the way. SCF was blessed to have a board consisting of men and women with more than 100 years of collective ministry service. Not only did these fine people work to define the vision and mission of SCF, but they provided credibility for the fledgling ministry. They were also able to open doors for recruiting and fundraising around the country.

Although many people served on the board, perhaps none made a larger impact than David. Months before he turned fifty years old, he was in a serious car accident that should have killed his entire family. But the Lord miraculously spared them. This event turned David's life around. He got involved in church, and immediately began to look for ways to use his remaining years for the Lord. "Whatever I do and will do," David said, "I can never repay the debt I owe God."

Convinced that the Lord wanted him to be more involved in missions, David joined the SCF board several months after we launched the mission. In time, he assumed the role of chairman. Not content to simply attend meetings and provide big picture direction for the ministry, David went out to visit the church planters where they lived and served. It was no easy task. The only way he could get to some remote places was on the back of a motorcycle. But the visits were so important to our church planters. Having their board chairman come to their houses and spend time getting to know them greatly encouraged them. David even took part on SCF survey teams as they prepared to send new teams into unreached areas.

"God has been gracious to use many people to be a blessing for missions in Indonesia," David said. "SCF has been used by the Lord to save souls. We're seeing what can happen when an organization has a clear vision, a dedicated executive, and a strong board. The role the Lord gave me was to be a part of strategic decision making. As a businessman, logic and tough decisions are part of my background. Sometimes mission people are too kind in a wrong way. The Lord put me in SCF to be a balancing factor."

Launching a mission endeavor to the Sundanese was a gigantic undertaking. Many people played a part in it, each one fulfilling the role that the Lord had specifically for him or her.

"God has been gracious to us," David said. "He tested us, and we succeeded because of our perseverance, sincerity in our prayers, and fellowship. One thing I have learned in my service with SCF is to be humble. If you hear the experiences and problems the church planters face in the field, I think, 'What have I done compared to them?' It is a real honor to be involved in this ministry with them."

CHAPTER 6

First Blossoms

"Has anyone explained to you who Christ is?" That's what I had asked Budi, the Sundanese school teacher I met out in a remote village. He was the first person in Indonesia to whom I presented the gospel. Even though he had seemed completely unmoved, when it came time to part, I had given him a Sundanese-language Bible.

The gospel is the power of God (Romans 1:16), yet it seems to be met by an apathetic response by the Sundanese. Why are they so unmoved? Is it that they don't understand the gospel when I explain it to them? Could it be that they simply have no interest in spiritual matters?

The fact is that many factors work against Muslims in general, and Sundanese in particular, to keep them from accepting the gospel. Their typical response is, "The different religions are like different rivers flowing to the same ocean." The Sundanese, as a whole, don't understand that the gospel is completely different from their current beliefs. The more the SCF church planters and I shared the gospel with them, the more we realized that unless God reached out and worked in their hearts, nothing would bring them to a saving faith in Christ.

Each day, SCF's church planters went out looking for people open to the gospel, people God had prepared. The church planters came upon one man who was quite ill. As they spoke with him, they could immediately see his interest. They shared the gospel with both him and his wife, and the couple accepted Christ that day. It was SCF's first fruit.

One night not long afterward, the ill man's wife rushed to Domu's house, her eyes brimming with tears. Her husband had a terrible nightmare, she said, as if he was hanging between life and death. He cried out the only thing he could remember: "Jesus save me!" Immediately he calmed down, and he passed away in peace. Since the man's family lived so far away, Sutrisno and another church planter prepared his body for burial the next day, as was the Sundanese custom[1]. When the man's extended family finally arrived, they were furious. They threw the church planters out of the village, exclaiming "Our father was a Muslim, and he will always be a Muslim!" Then they buried the man in accordance with their Islamic traditions. It didn't matter. We knew the man was already with the Lord.

A man named Ubai was close to believing in Christ when the Lord brought him across our path. Of all the children in his family, he was the most committed to his Islamic faith. Now, at age 32, he was a respected teacher at the Madrasah, a Muslim boarding school, where he taught 120 children.

One day, as Ubai rode a city bus in the capital city of Jakarta, he met a man who told him about Christ. The gospel

---

[1] According to both the Sundanese and Islamic burial rites, a body must be interred within 24 hours of death.

message appealed to Ubai because the Qur'an does not offer an assurance of salvation, not even for those who diligently perform the Islamic rituals. Ubai analyzed his own faith, and he found it wanting. So he sought out more information by going to the man's house on several other occasions. Each time he returned to his village, which was many hours outside of town, and pondered what he had just heard. After not visiting this man for almost a year, Ubai again tried to contact him, only to discover that the man had moved to another city. Although the current tenant didn't know where Ubai could find the man, he did know of someone else who could answer his questions about Jesus. So the man brought Ubai to SCF's office. Domu greeted him and shared the gospel. Ubai bowed his head and prayed to receive Jesus as his Savior.

Over the next five months, Domu faithfully taught Ubai, and Ubai grew quickly in his love for Jesus. His presence strengthened the faith of other Sundanese believers when they met together for Bible Study. Ubai still had not taken the step of letting anyone know that he had become a Christian because he feared the repercussions he would face. He was, after all, an Islamic teacher in his village. We all felt it best that he witness to his family through a changed life before sharing the gospel with others through words. Often in the middle of the night, he would awaken and read the Bible, as well as tracts he kept hidden in the bedroom closet. Ubai and SCF were starting a micro-credit scheme to help the economic status of several people in his village. It would also allow the church planters to visit the village without arousing suspicion.

One Saturday, Domu invited me over to have lunch with Ubai. I was struck by the joy of the Lord so evident on Ubai's countenance. But two days later, Ubai's wife called and said her husband was extremely sick and needed to go to the hospital. Domu went to the village to pick up Ubai, and he brought him to the hospital in the nearby town. For the past several days he had been vomiting and sick with diarrhea. The poor fellow was severely dehydrated, had a weak pulse, and his internal organs had started to fail. But Ubai had not received medical attention soon enough. After two days in the hospital, he passed into God's presence. It was a shocking turn of events. When Domu took Ubai's body back home, the village went into hysterics. Family and friends had no idea what had happened. In respect of Ubai, many Muslim men and Islamic school children also came out for the funeral.

For us, it was a crushing turn of events. We had such high hopes for that young man. In our minds, he could be leader of the future church among the Sundanese. But God's plans are not our plans. Now all we could pray was that Ubai's closet full of books and a Bible would be discovered and read by people in his village.

Ubai was the third new believer the Lord had called home soon after coming to Christ. I remember praying on this occassion, "Lord, if You want us to plant churches here, You must keep the congregation around longer and stop taking them away from us!"

Step-by-step, momentum built as church planters joined us and gained experience in reaching out to Muslims. And the Lord continued to lead them to people ready to listen. The success was tied to a concerted prayer effort. Every week we met on the hillside outside of town to fast and pray for an entire day. We did this for years, and God answered our prayers.

The Lord raised up our most fruitful church plant on that very hillside. It began with a small, poorly educated Sundanese woman named Kalimah. Although she was married to a nominal Christian of Batak ethnicity, Kalimah held to her Islamic beliefs. But she was not content. For fifteen years, Kalimah had watched Christian families, and seen how happy they were together. They stood in stark contrast to the families she knew in the Sundanese community. The more Kalimah saw, the more she wanted to learn about Jesus. After several meeting with the SCF church planter, she put her faith in Christ and asked to be baptized in her husband's church (HKBP). She was, along with her children, and afterwards they had a thanksgiving service at their house. Domu, also a Batak, was asked to speak. "When someone believes in Jesus, it is only the beginning," he said. "Many trials will come, for it is not easy to follow Christ."

Domu was right. Trials came that very night. Villagers angry over Kalimah's conversion stormed her house, fully intending to burn it down. In such villages, people are frequently related to one another. When one person does something considered dishonorable—such as becoming a Christian—it brings shame on the entire extended family. Kalimah's furious uncle came with the mob, and he brought his machete along. He grabbed Kalimah and held the machete to her throat. "Return to Islam!" he ordered.

"Go ahead and kill me," Kalimah retorted. "My heart is set on Christ and I will never deny Him."

The villagers did not burn Kalimah's house, nor did her uncle kill her. Instead, they dragged her off to the village office and demanded to know who had forced her to become a Christian. "My husband did not force me," Kalimah stated. "The desire to follow Christ came from my own heart. I have seen how Christians love one another, and I want to live like that. Even if you kill me tonight, I will not return to Islam."

A village official ordered Kalimah released. Since she had become a Christian by her own initiative, he said, there was no case against her.

But her trials had just begun.

Kalimah's family disowned her. Her widowed mother denied her any inheritance then she ordered Kalimah to buy the house where her family lived. That house had previously been given to Kalimah by her father. When her mother insisted these were her family's wishes, Kalimah's response was simple: "Mom, I don't feel I have lost anything. I'm fine with everything being taken away, because I will receive my greatest inheritance when I get to heaven."

Kalimah and her husband moved out of their house, and her extended family disowned her. Although they still lived in the village, the other villagers snubbed and ignored them. Owners of the small shops scattered throughout the village would no longer sell her food staples—sugar, rice, water, and spices—because the religious leaders warned them that it was *haram* (forbidden) to do business with a Christian. In exasperation, Kalimah exclaimed to one shop owner, "Didn't you buy the food supplies you are selling from a Chinese businessman in the city? And wasn't he a Christian? If you were able to do business with him, why can't you do business with me?" The shop owner couldn't argue with her logic. So she allowed Kalimah to buy at her shop once again.

Despite everything, Kalimah's faith in Christ filled her heart with joy. It showed in the way she lived her life. After two years, her family came to her and restored the severed relationship. They even returned her inheritance to her. Over the years, we have found that to nearly always be the case. As new believers have demonstrated consistent testimonies by being good neighbors and honoring their parents, they have been able to work their way back into the life of the community.

In December of 1998, after eight years of learning how to reach out to the Sundanese people, we held our first baptism. We baptized nine people that day. The following year, we baptized nineteen more. As the Lord raised up more church planters to join with us, we watched as the seeds SCF had planted begin to produce fruit. When the ministry reached a count of eight church planters, it seemed to take on new momentum and enthusiasm. Now we had more than twenty. We had figured out how to recruit new church planters, and also how to train them in appropriate ways to reach Sundanese Muslims. We were past the crucial period.

At the end of 1999, we brought all the church planters to the beach for a picnic, a time of refreshment after all their hard work and faithful service. They had certainly earned it. They had just finished their Christmas outreaches in the villages where hundreds of Muslims were exposed to the gospel. Domu and I sat back watching them enjoying themselves and each other.

"Just see how far SCF has come!" we said to each other. Great joy filled our hearts at all the Lord had done. Yet our words were filled with a sense of blessed expectation for all that was still to come. The Lord would use the SCF church planters in remarkable ways in the coming years. Of that we were certain.

CHAPTER 7

Threat of Locusts

"Matt," Domu said over the phone on the morning of January 3. "We need to talk."

"What's up?" The urgency in his voice concerned me.

"When I opened up the office today after our Christmas break, there was a letter here for us. Let me read it to you."

To: Attorney General of Indonesia

Cc: Chairman of the Islamic Council of Indonesia

Date: 10 December 1999

Dear Sir,

I am writing to inform you that in the past few years there has been a movement carried out by Christians that is illegal as it seeks to cause Muslims to become apostates and embrace Christianity. In other words they are trying to Christianize our Muslim population.

Already there have been several Muslims who have committed apostasy and have become Christians.

This same sort of thing has occurred in West Sumatra by Western missionaries which has caused the Muslims in Padang to become tense. The Attorney General's investigation in Padang resulted in the perpetrators being sentenced to 2-6 years in prison. We ask the willingness of you and your staff to investigate this new movement and if proved guilty, to put an end to their activities. The leaders behind it must be sentenced under the law.

The headquarters is in a two story building in ...[1] One floor is used for an office while the other is the classroom. Every day they teach strategizes to Christianize Muslims. The building is located at ...

The training is run by Domu. The other teachers are Matt Kirkas and Lerry, both of whom are Americans. The group goes by the name of Sundanese Christian Fellowship. They are a branch of another organization led by Faisal Iman.

I hope that this information will be carefully investigated because this training has already graduated many people who are infiltrating many *madrasah* throughout Indonesia. This group has also built relationships with people in other provinces of Indonesia. Concerning the finances of this organization, you will need to check with the bank to determine the source of these funds.

---

[1] Address withheld for security reasons.

We are ready to wage Jihad against them and fight them after Idul Fitri (January 8-9). Now we are collecting the addresses of these people to make it easier to move against them. But we ask that you investigate this matter first.

Wassalam. Drs. Engkos Kaswita, SH.

One of our worst nightmares had just come true! Although we were not sending church planters into Muslim boarding schools, the letter did expose our evangelistic work among the Muslims of West Java. An important part of ministering successfully in a Muslim country is not drawing attention to yourself. That's the only way the ministry can move forward without state interference or mob threats. Obviously, that was no longer possible. Someone had reported our activities.

We were just three weeks away from our next training session, and mere days from our January 8 preparation deadline. As it happened, January 8 was also the end of the Muslim fasting month, which meant Muslims would be celebrating with even greater religious fervor than usual. All the excitement we had experienced at the end of 1999 evaporated like water under the tropical sun. We would have to drop everything and get ready for a "visit" from government officials. We quickly destroyed files, scrubbed our computers free of data, and moved every piece of evangelistic literature off site. Even as we scrambled to finish in time, we brought the matter before the Lord. And in the midst of the wild flurry of activity, a sense of peace covered us. We knew we had the Lord's protection. There was nothing to do but wait.

We decided to go ahead with our yearly planning meeting, set to begin in two days. We brought all the church planters together outside of town, in a villa owned by a Christian friend of SCF. And in a spirit of unity, we came before God and asked Him to be with us.

At this meeting, I met two new workers. Imagine how they must have felt stepping into such a situation! I was impressed that they didn't jump on the first bus out of town and never look back. Obviously, their calling to serve the Lord in that place was firm. Years later, Abdi, one of the worker, told me, "I asked myself whether or not I wanted to go forward with my commitment to serve with SCF. But I decided not to let my heart be persuaded by the current situation. I was prepared to face whatever might arise. I believed that the ministry was from the Lord and that He had called me to it. Praise God that I made the correct decision!"

On January 8 and 9, as Muslims celebrated the end of Ramadan, groups of young men paraded around the neighborhood all night long beating a drum. Each time they passed our house, I expected them to come for us. Yet all of us with SCF decided we would not put our trust in human strength, nor rely on "connections" in the government. We would trust in the Lord alone. The Psalms teach that *"The eyes of the Lord are on the righteous and his ears are attentive to their cry"* (Psalm 34:15).

Time passed. We waited and we watched, but still no "visit" from either government officials or any Muslim group. We badly needed to restart our training program. Our new church planters must be prepared for the work that awaited them. The leadership of SCF gathered in my house to discuss reopening the program. While we were meeting, a fax came for me from Faisal Iman, chairman of SCF's Board of Directors. It was a copy of a letter Faisal had just received.

Date: 12 Januari 2000

To: Chairman of The Islamic Council of Indonesia

Cc: Attorney General of Indonesia

Dear Sir,

Following up on our first letter, we have received confirmation that the training program has been temporarily suspended. We are told that the training will begin again once the situation is safe. We must be careful not to fail in our task. If you want to apprehend more of the leaders behind this work, take action against:

Matt Kirkas

Address and Phone: …

Faisal Iman

Address and Phone: …

There are still 2 other names and addresses that we will send to you. Once they begin their activities, move in and destroy them.

For the moment that is what we have to report. We are preparing our forces to act swiftly.

Wassalam. Drs. Engkos Kaswita, SH.

CC: Attorney General in Jakarta

Needless to say, the fax ended our discussion on reopening the training. Whoever was behind these threats knew where I lived. What was more, they were preparing to attack. I couldn't help but wonder, *What will happen to my wife and children? Should we move out and lie low in some other place?*

At times of great uncertainty, it's easy to react in self-preservation. Our family had both the means and the opportunity to relocate to a safe location in another city, even outside the country. But I was a leader in the work alongside Domu. If I were to flee and leave these men and women behind, how would I ever be able to lead them again?

Working in partnership with the Indonesians required that we make major decisions only after consulting with them. So Domu and I sat down and discussed this most recent threat. "I want you to know that my family is committed to staying put as long as it doesn't make things more difficult for you and the other Indonesians," I told him. "I realize that having a foreigner around can bring unwanted publicity and further complicate this escalating situation. So I need you to tell us what to do. If you ever feel that my presence here is making the situation worse, let me know and we will lie low somewhere else. But until then, you can count on us to be right here beside you."

Since we had no evidence that copies of the letters had actually been sent to the authorities, we agreed not to report the matter. Anyway, had we shown them the letters, it would have alerted them to our activities and they would certainly have started to investigate. Nor would we attempt to find protection through Christians in the government. We committed ourselves to asking the Lord alone for protection. His name and glory were more important to all of us in SCF than our own safety.

The backdrop to all of this was that Muslim fundamentalists and elements of the military were creating chaos in an attempt to reassert themselves in national politics. They had recently burned churches and Christian's houses on one of the islands. The headline in one newspaper declared that "provocateurs" had already infiltrated the city and were trying to cause riots. Perhaps the letters we received were part of an attempt to rile people up and create religious tensions and rioting. Also, a rumor spread that a pig's head was found in a mosque. The Indonesian president accused certain military elements of trying to cause disturbances.

In the middle of February, the president gained control of the military and things began to calm. Over the next weeks, we prayed and waited for something to happen. Nothing did. Slowly we again started active outreach.

Not one of us had the slightest doubt that it was the Lord Himself who had protected us.

CHAPTER 8

A Hearty Plant

Memet awoke with a start. Squinting, he struggled to orient himself to his surroundings. Yes, yes, he was still in his bedroom. He breathed a sigh of relief.

For years Memet had practiced his craft of shamanism[1] in the village. People came to him looking for solutions to their problems. He helped them find spouses, secure employment, even recover from illnesses—always by calling on the spirits to intercede. But now at night, these spirits had started to torment him in his dreams. This night was different, though. This night Memet dreamed that two people would be coming to visit him the next day. Since he had so clearly seen their faces in his dream, he knew he would recognize them.

Later the next day, two of SCF's church planters stopped by Memet's house in the village. Memet knew these were the men from his dream. They struck up a conversation which the

---

[1] Shamanism is the folk beliefs in which the practitioner (shaman) maintains harmony in between the seen and unseen world. People who adhere to folk religions believe that things that happen in their lives have causes in the spiritual realm. A shaman serves to assist people as they try to overcome these problems.

church planters were able to direct towards the gospel. Memet's response to hearing the good news was encouraging, so the church planters continued to visit. Memet told them about his nightmares and how spirits tormented throughout the night. As he heard more about Christ and His power, Memet knew he was in desperate need of a Savior. He put his faith in Jesus and was baptized in 1999. "Once I received the Lord," Memet says, "I was set free!"

In early 2000, Abdi came along to visit Memet. Abdi was surprised at what he found. Instead of a clean, well-groomed man who loved the Lord, he saw a man still plying his trade of shamanism. Memet lived in the middle of a field. His hair was long and unkempt, and it appeared he had not bathed in quite some time. Scattered around his house were many of the items he had used in his shamanistic ceremonies to assist people who came to him for help.

"What are these?" Abdi asked as he picked up a couple of thing strewn across Memet's table.

"Oh those," Memet said with a shrug. "They are just some things I use to help people in this area who come to me."

"What kind of help do they need?"

"Many people have problems," Memet said. "Some need to find a job. Others want their business to be blessed. Yesterday, someone needed my help because his enemy was trying to kill him."

"How can you protect him?" Abdi asked. "You are not very big or strong."

"Well, it was not that kind of help he needed," Memet said. "You see, another shaman used black magic to try to kill him. He wanted me to take the power out of that magic."

Memet obviously had no more than a rudimentary understanding of his new faith. Right then and there, Abdi committed himself to visiting Memet often, and to teaching him God's Word. So Abdi came back three or four times each week. Because Memet was poor, he brought two liters of rice along with him, and some instant noodles, too. They cooked together. After sharing a meal with Memet and his family, Abdi, reading to the illiterate man, taught from the Bible.

But change was slow to come. Sometimes when Abdi came to visit, Memet would stop working in his field and sit with him. But other times, Memet kept right on with his work, seemingly completely disinterested in Abdi's visit. Whenever Memet did show interest, Abdi worked to teach him to read. It was his hope that at some point Memet would be able to read the Bible for himself.

Then in 2002, a surprising and sudden change occurred. Memet was at work in the field when he saw Abdi approaching his house. Immediately he hurried in and sat down with his visitor. They talked of this and that, then their conversation turned to reading. Memet had dropped out of school in second grade. (That was not at all unusual for people in the village. Once children learned their letters and numbers, they often stopped their formal schooling and went back to work in the fields. After years of not reading, most of them lost even that little bit they had learned and slipped back into illiteracy.) Abdi gave Memet a verse and asked if he could read it. Although Memet stumbled through the text, he did manage to read it almost correctly. The reading lessons had actually paid off. On another visit, Abdi brought Memet reading glasses, which helped immensely. When Memet put the glasses on, he started reading as though he had been doing it his entire life.

As Memet read the Bible for himself, his life began to change in remarkable ways. People noticed. More villagers than ever came to him for help with their problems, but he told them he was no longer involved in spirit practices. "Jesus Christ is the true God, and only He can help You," he quickly added. Instead of calling on the spirits, Memet prayed for each person in Jesus' name. His prayers were answered, so still more people came. They wanted Memet to pray for them, too.

One day, Memet's father-in-law came to visit, and he brought several other men with him. It turned out that they were all shamans. "Memet," his father-in-law said, "we came here today to challenge you to a duel of magic. We will find out today whose magic is stronger."

"Why do you want to do that?" Memet exclaimed. "We are all family."

"For the past several months, people have not been coming to me or to these others for help," Memet's father-in-law said. "They have been coming to you instead. We want to show them our powers are stronger than yours so they will return to us."

"I do not have magical powers anymore," Memet said. "I only have the Lord Jesus Christ. And I will not test the Lord in that way."

Eyes flashing, one of the other shamans pronounced, "Whether you have powers or not, we are going to battle you!" Immediately, they all began to use *santet*[2] against Memet. It was clear that they wanted to see him dead.

One night, an explosion above Memet's house awakened his family. He got up from his bed and knelt down to pray. He was fully aware of the power of black magic, but he committed the battle to the Lord and asked for God's protection.

A week later, three of the shamans came to Memet and confessed that his power was greater than theirs. "As I already told you, I don't have any magic powers," Memet insisted. "I only have the Lord Jesus." Even so, the three admitted defeat and asked forgiveness before going on their way. But the last shaman, Jagat, refused to stop the battle. He was from a village

---

[2] *Santet* is a form of black magic employed to harm another person from a distance.

on the south coast of Java where they worshipped Nyai Roro Kidul, goddess of the South Sea. Jagat was such a powerful shaman that he was considered the leader of the shamans in that area. Before Memet knew Christ, he considered Jagat his leader, too.

Soon Memet fell so ill that he was unable to do anything. He called for Abdi and some other SCF church planters to come to his house and pray for him. They prayed and they fasted, but Memet grew worse. After a week, he could no longer eat anything, or even get up from his bed. It was as if a snake had wrapped itself around his body and was squeezing the life out of him. Once again Memet sent for Abdi and his friends. He pleaded with them to pray. "A snake spirit torments me," he cried. "It is like the snake is staring right into my eyes!" The men fell before the Lord and prayed for Memet. Claiming God's promises, they prayed some more. And the Lord gave them victory. Memet finally fell asleep, and by morning, he was back to normal.

Three weeks later, someone came to Memet's house with the news that Jagat had died. They said he had been standing along the south coast, offering a pig's head as a sacrifice to Nyai Roro Kidul, when a huge wave came up suddenly and pulled him under.

News of Jagat's death spread quickly. At the same time, more and more people heard about what the Lord was doing in Memet's life. Things began to happen in his wife, Fatimah's, life as well. Fatimah had not responded well to Abdi's ministry to their family. She viewed him with cynicism that turned into outright hatred. When Abdi came to the house to instruct them in the Bible, Fatimah quickly found an excuse to avoid staying in the room with him. Despite the tension, Abdi always treated

Fatimah warmly. He did everything he could to allay her concerns. It was Abdi's love for the family that finally won her over. She put her faith in Christ, just as her husband had done. Immediately she began to witness to others. She sold kitchen utensils door to door in her village and in several other villages as well. As she peddled her wares, she shared how she had come to know Christ with everyone who would listen.

But not everyone was happy about Fatimah's newfound faith. One lady reported her to the local authorities. Fatimah was told to appear at the village office to meet with the village chief, who was investigating the matter. As in numerous other villages, many people in Memet and Fatimah's village were related to one another. Even the village chief was part of her extended family. That meant he was duty-bound to protect the family's reputation against such a dishonorable accusation as one of their own becoming a Christian. Tiny Fatimah, who stood no more than five feet tall, strode right into the village office and stood undaunted before the chief's desk. "I was told you asked to see me," she said.

"Take a seat," the village chief snapped. Adorned in his official uniform, his badges shining on his chest, he peered down at her from across his desk. "I heard you have become a Christian. Is it true?"

Fatimah, her head held high, answered, "That's right. I have become a Christian."

The village chief was taken aback by her directness. But he quickly recovered himself and pressed, "If you are a Christian, prove it to me. Everyone says all Christians can sing, so you sing for me. Right now."

Fatimah was outgoing and not at all concerned about what people might think of her singing. She opened her mouth and, to the traditional Sundanese musical rhythm, she belted out an off-key rendition of a song she learned in the church meeting: *"Gusti Allah miasih umat manusa, Mijalma jadi manusa sejati, Ngorbankeun salira-Na, Pupus dina kai palang, Eta buktos kaasih Pangeran."*[3]

For a moment, the village chief could do nothing but stare. He never suspected that Fatimah actually *could* sing. When she finished, he exclaimed, "You *can* sing! I had no idea! That must mean that you really are a Christian."

The village chief's reaction stirred up the fires of Fatimah's boldness. "That's right! Just as I told you, I have become a Christian. That is why you should come with me to church on Sunday."

The village chief quickly dismissed her. Fatimah was not coerced again. Because she dared to stand up to the village chief, many more in the village heard about Christ, and how Memet and Fatimah now followed Him.

---

[3] Translation of the song is, "The Lord God loves mankind, so he took on flesh becoming a true man. Sacrificing Himself, He died on the cross. That is the proof of the Lord's love."

CHAPTER 9

Blossoms to First Fruits

From childhood, Saladin had often withdrawn to a quiet place to meditate on the Qur'an, or had sought out an *ustad*[1] who he hoped could lead him to an assurance about life after death. But nothing he tried had ever provided him with the assurance he longed for. Then one day, Saladin happened upon a sermon broadcast on a Christian radio station. To his surprise, it was not filled with attacks and insults on Islam. Instead, it rang of wisdom and comforting words. It inspired hope in him. That sermon sparked such great curiosity in Saladin that he absolutely *had* to learn more about Christianity.

When news that Memet and Fatimah, who lived in the next village, had become Christians, Saladin determined he would meet them. Maybe they would be able to lead him to the assurance he so desperately sought. Not long afterwards, Fatimah stopped by Saladin's house with the kitchen utensils she was selling door to door. Finally, a chance to meet the infamous Fatimah! Finally, a chance to talk to a real Christian!

"I want to follow you, Fatimah," Saladin told her.

---

[1] A teacher of Islam

"Follow me?" Fatimah shook her head. "No, no. Do not follow me. That would be much too dangerous. But if you want to learn about Jesus, come to our meeting on Thursday night."

Saladin had no idea what they did at those meetings, so he sent his wife to observe while he stayed home. So on Thursday night, Fatimah took Saladin's wife to the house church meeting. The next day, Abdi sought out Saladin at his house. Abdi explained to both Saladin and his wife who Jesus Christ is, and what it means to be His follower. They listened carefully, for God had been preparing them.

After explaining the good news, Abdi looked Saladin straight in the eye and said, "This is your soul we are talking about. It's up to you whether or not you want to follow Jesus. But don't wait until it's too late. We don't know when our lives will end, and you are already on in years." Both Saladin and his wife responded to Abdi's challenge. They received Jesus as Savior and were baptized on April 23, 2003.

In Indonesian villages, neighbors keep watch on one another to ensure that no one strays from the community's will. Because Abdi often visited Saladin at his home, the neighbors saw, and they began to ask questions. Why did Saladin have a Christian friend? What were the two of them doing together? Rumors spread that Saladin and his wife had become Christians. Then at one Friday prayers, an announcement was made at the mosque: "Be on your guard. Saladin has already left Islam and become a Christian." The situation escalated so quickly that Abdi had to cut back the frequency of his visits to Saladin's house.

Finally the neighborhood leaders came to Saladin and confronted him. Were the rumors true? Had he really become a

Christian? They didn't actually forbid him from believing in Christ, but they did warn him: "We want to remind you that in this village there are no Christians. If you were to die, no one will bury your body." Surely, they thought, that would scare Saladin back to Islam.

It did not. Saladin was unmoved. He simply replied, "Don't worry about me. The Christians will come and take care of me." Saladin stood firm, insisting that he would not return to Islam. But from that day on, the village leaders forbid anyone from doing business with him.

Saladin's sundry shop went bankrupt. Neighbors were forced to keep their distance from him. Under the crushing isolation, Saladin's faith began to waver. But not his wife's faith. She remained steadfast, and the Lord used her to strengthen her husband. She encouraged him, saying, "We have already started down this path. We cannot and we will not retreat now."

But pressure from the community didn't let up. So Saladin and his wife moved out of the village. An Indonesian Christian[2] had a plot of farm land in that area and he allowed them to move there. In the middle of the property was a simple shelter. It was run down, unused for a long time. It had no walls and many of the tiles were missing from the roof. But Saladin managed to fashion bamboo mats to use for walls, and he repaired the holes in the roof. Finally, he and his wife had a new place to call home.

---

[2] In Indonesia there are several ethnic groups that have embraced the gospel since the 1800s. Over time, these groups have migrated throughout the country and are living amid majority Muslim people of different ethnicity.

Abdi continued to disciple Saladin and his wife. Their great desire was for their grown children and their children's spouses to also know the Lord, so they started a group to teach them the Bible. Then Saladin fell under spiritual attack. Suddenly one evening, he saw a ball of fire appear before him. It attacked him and made him fall ill. He was in such critical condition that it looked as if he would surely die. He lay in bed in great pain, sweating profusely and with bloodshot eyes.

At the very same time, Abdi lay in his bed dreaming that he was wrestling with an evil spirit. A knock at the door awakened him. It was Saladin's wife. She had run to him in a panic.

Despite his weakness, Saladin cried out to God, "Lord, I commit this situation and my life to You." Throughout the night he wrestled with the ball of fire. From ten in the evening until four in the morning, his condition grew worse. Abdi and Fatimah continued to pray for him. Finally, in the early hours of the morning, the ball of fire disappeared.

It was not until a year and a half later that Saladin discovered what had happened that night. After Abdi's neighbor came to faith through Abdi's ministry, he confessed that he had been given money to hire a shaman to use black magic to kill both Abdi and Saladin. And yet, it was through that difficult and terrifying event that Saladin learned the blessed truth that the Lord would protect him in every situation. Now he can face all future struggles with confidence.

Saladin and Memet's families serve as elders of the house church. Because they are known as Christians, many Muslims come to them to seek their counsel and to ask for prayers when they face difficult situations. Memet tells them, "I can do nothing to help you, but I know one who can. His name is Isa Al-Masih.[3] Let's pray and ask His advice in this matter."

The Lord continues to use these two families to bring many to faith—Saladin's children and sons-in-law are now Christians. The Indonesian church purposely reaches out to others in the area to help them with their physical and spiritual needs. Demonstrating Christ's love in such practical ways provides the basis of their testimony to the Muslims around them. Practical acts of caring are an important part of the church's testimony in the world. Demonstrating the love of Jesus in such real ways opens people's hearts to hear the gospel.

Karta is an excellent example. Cataracts in both his eyes had left Karta unable to see clearly for two years. He had spent a good deal of his own money, yet his vision did not improve.

---

[3] The Muslim name for Jesus

The church prayed asking God to heal Karta's eyes, but still he could barely see. So Abdi and Memet took him to see a doctor, and on the way home they explained the gospel to him. Because of the love the church demonstrated in such practical and caring ways, Karta turned to Christ.

Karta was a believer, but the church still was not satisfied. They wanted him to be able to see. So they worked and worked until they raised enough money for the operation he needed. The surgery was successful. Even so, Karta's neighbors turned against him and his family. When they saw that he was not attending the mosque any more for Friday prayers, they realized that he had become a Christian. Even though Karta and his family were rejected, they stayed faithful to Christ and continued to grow. Karta and his wife actively shared the gospel with others.

Karta told Abdi, "Even in my old age, I want to be used by the Lord. I want to be found faithful by Him."

CHAPTER 10

From a Garden Plant to a Tree

"Bambang, praise the Lord!" Satrio exclaimed. "Domu passed the news on to me that you have been accepted as a new church planter with SCF."

"That's right," Bambang answered. "But I have not decided for sure whether or not I will join."

Satrio stared at his friend in surprise. "Why not?"

"If I decide to work among the Sundanese, I don't want to quit half way into it. I want to make sure I will be faithful to the end. So I am asking God for a sign to confirm my calling."

It was while Bambang was praying over his decision that he met Pak Haji,[1] a man suffering from the effects of a stroke that had left him partially paralyzed. As is the custom of all SCF's church planters, Bambang directed the conversation to Christ. He told Pak Haji that salvation could be found only in Him.

---

[1] Pak Haji is the honorific title given to one who has completed the Hajj pilgrimage to Mecca as prescribed by Islam.

That day, Bambang had the privilege of leading Pak Haji in a prayer to receive Jesus. Because Pak Haji was afraid of what would happen if his neighbors found out about his new faith too soon, he declined the invitation to go to church with Bambang. Pak Haji passed away soon after, but his response was the sign Bambang needed. He and his family joined SCF.

Without a doubt, Bambang had the gift of evangelism. During the six-month course in church planting, he won another two Sundanese Muslims to the Lord and saw them baptized. After he completed his training, SCF asked him to spearhead church planting in a new area that was completely closed to Christians. Once a church had attempted to hold a Sunday service to minister to the non-Sundanese Christians in the area, but the Muslim leaders would not permit it.

In June 2002, Bambang and his family moved to that resistant place. But after three months with nothing to show for his efforts, he was ready to quit. "In training, I baptized two new believers," he said. "But here I am not finding any fruit." Thoroughly dejected, Bambang committed himself to a month of fasting. He prayed, "Did You truly send me here, Lord, or was it simply what my leader Domu wanted?"

During this time, Bambang was also preparing for a new team member to join him. He found a house for the new worker and paid the rent, then he went to work overseeing its renovations. But one time while he was supervising the repairs on the house, he felt a voice in his heart telling him to go out to the street. Obeying that leading, he walked down a narrow pathway, just wide enough for foot traffic. The 80-yard trip took him past several houses in the densely populated area. When he reached the main street, he looked around, confused. The street seemed deserted. Then a man appeared, walked right up to him and called out a greeting. "What are you looking for?" the man asked.

Bambang said, "I am overseeing renovations down this path."

Introducing himself as Rahmat, the man suggested that they find shade on the veranda of someone's house. Rahmat poured out the difficulties he was facing. "I cannot return home because debt collectors are after me. I took some things on consignment to sell. Then I recruited several of my friends to help me sell from house to house. But one of the salesmen took off with everything. Now I can't pay what I owe, and debt collectors are threatening me. I cannot go back home to my wife and kids because my house is being watched."

"Since you are in trouble, I want to pray for you," Bambang said. Afterwards, he gave Rahmat his address. "If you don't have any place to stay, come and stay with me. My home is always open to you."

Later that evening Rahmat did come over. And for the next several days, he continued to come by. Each time, Bambang shared more of the gospel with him. On the sixth day, Rahmat said, "I want to learn more about Christ. I don't care what other people think." So they began to study the Bible together.

After three months of Bible study, Rahmat brought his friend Abdullah over to meet Bambang. Abdullah was an imam who often led prayers in a nearby mosque. He was also the village secretary, a position second only in prestige to village chief. But then Abdullah's life took a turn for the worse. His family left him. Dejected, Abdullah considered killing himself. Then he dreamed that his former religious teacher came to him and said, "Do not fear or lose heart. You need to know that Isa

Al-Masih is Lord and Savior." Strange! In the Qur'an, Isa Al-Masih is just a prophet, not the Savior. Abdullah awoke from his dream with a start. All he could think was, *Where can I find information about Isa Al-Masih?*

"Isa Al-Masih is Lord and Savior." Abdullah could not get those words out of his mind. The next day, he met his friend Rahmat. Rahmat scrutinized him, then asked if he was well. Reluctantly, Abdullah mentioned his problems at home. It was hard to do because Muslims believe that when their lives take a turn for the worse, it's a sign that they are cursed by God. But Abdullah was desperate. He leaned close and whispered, "I had a dream last night. I dreamed that I had just finished my prayers at the mosque. Although my heart was heavy because of my problems at home, I met my former teacher, the one who taught me to recite the Qur'an. He told me that Isa Al-Masih is the Savior!"

"I'm not sure what to tell you," Rahmat said. "I don't understand much about Isa Al-Masih either, but I do know a really good Christian who is teaching me the Bible."

That night, Bambang was surprised to find two men at the door. Abdullah explained that he also wanted to learn the Bible. So for three days each week, Bambang taught the two men starting with creation and the fall. He wanted to be certain they understood that no person can be saved by performing good deeds or fulfilling religious obligations. The reason Isa Al-Masih came into the world was to pay the debt for our sins. After a few months of study together, both Rahmat and Abdullah put their faith in Christ and were baptized.

Because Abdullah was a community leader, his new faith brought many problems. He no longer attended Friday prayers at the mosque. Instead, he and Rahmat would go to Bambang's house on Fridays for a time of prayer, fasting, and Bible study. At first, the villagers didn't seem to notice. But eventually, they started asking why Abdullah was always away on Friday at prayer time rather than leading the prayers at the mosque as he should be doing.

Abdullah had not yet openly confessed his new faith in Christ. When people asked him why he no longer prayed at the mosque, he made excuses. He may have been reluctant to make his faith in Christ known, but God was not the least bit reluctant. Somehow Abdullah got a shirt with the symbol of a cross on it. A young man in the village saw him wearing that shirt and shouted, "Abdullah, that is a Christian shirt! It has a cross on it." Abdullah was taken aback. He didn't know how to answer. He hurried back to the place where he had been living, but before long, eight village leaders appeared at his door. They barged in, intending to interrogate him. But before they began, Abdullah offered to make them coffee. Actually, he just needed to get alone for a moment. Standing over coffee in his kitchen, he prayed and asked God for strength and wisdom to explain his faith to the angry men outside.

It didn't take long for the interrogation to begin. As soon as Abdullah handed the coffee around, Pak Ustad,[2] the village's Muslim leader, began. "Abdullah, we have noticed that on Friday you are no longer joining us for prayers at the mosque. Now we hear that you wore a shirt with a cross on it."

Abdullah could not possibly explain his way out of this situation. So he mustered his courage and answered, "I know

---

[2] Pak Ustad is the respectful address for a Muslim teacher.

what you are thinking, and you are right. I am now a Christian. It is the choice I made."

Immediately the men demanded that Abdullah tell them who coerced him into such a decision. But Abdullah insisted that no one forced him to believe in Christ. Then he told them about his dream. "That dream is what caused me to make this decision."

"If you say you are a Christian, that means you are an apostate from Islam," one of the men accused. "How much did the Christians pay you to leave Islam?"

In spite of his lowly economic status, Abdullah dared to answer, "I am not looking for anything in this world. What I seek is salvation. The important thing is that I know what will happen to me after I die. That is why I believe in Isa Al-Masih, just as I was told in my dream."

"If that is the case, have you determined that you will never return to Islam?" asked Pak Ustad.

"Yes, that is my decision," Abdullah answered. "I will never return to Islam."

Tears filled Pak Ustad's eyes and he began to weep. "Abdullah. You are the one I hoped would replace me at the mosque."

"Let another one of the other young men take my place."

None of their pleas were reaching Abdullah's heart. The village leaders could see that. Angry and frustrated, their mood changed. Their faces hard and their words as cutting as shards of broken glass, they issued an ultimatum: "Within one week,

Abdullah, you must be gone from this place." Then they turned their backs on him and left.

Immediately Abdullah sought out Bambang. He was at home when Abdullah arrived, meeting with other SCF church planters. They all turned their attention to Abdullah. First they informed him of his rights. Abdullah was born in that village. He owned his house there. So the village leaders had absolutely no basis on which to evict him. The second thing they did was to pray with him.

As the week-long deadline approached, the village leaders returned to Abdullah's house. "I decided not to move out of the village," Abdullah told them. But instead of evicting him, the leaders merely warned him not to share his Christian faith with others. Evidently, they didn't know Abdullah very well!

As Abdullah continued to grow in his faith, he displayed the gifts of teaching and shepherding. In the house church meeting, he took an active role in pastoring the flock. And he went out to visit other Sundanese people and to tell them about Jesus. One afternoon, Bambang arrived at Abdullah's house to find him in front of a small white board explaining the gospel to a Muslim man. God had indeed raised up Abdullah to serve Him in that place.

Because he firmly believed that God was at work in that place, Bambang continued to reach out to other families. One afternoon in 2005, he gathered the members of his church planting team together to spend the day in prayer for their ministry. They decided to meet at a friend's house where they could pray freely. While they were waiting for the final team member to arrive, a man approached the open door of the house and said, "*Assalamu alaikum.*" Bambang promptly replied, *"Wa alaikum assalaam,* please come in."[3] The man entered the house, then bowed down on the floor before Bambang and his teammates. He said, "I am so sorry for disturbing you."

"Please don't bow to us," Bambang graciously told the man. "Come, sit here next to me."

"I will just sit on the floor," the man replied.

"We are all God's creatures," Bambang said gently. "There is no difference between any of us. Sit on the sofa next to me. I insist. And tell me, what is the problem?"

The man, whose name was Cecep, poured out his story. He had moved to the capital city of Jakarta to work as a driver for a businessman's family. But while he was there, he fell ill and for eight months couldn't work. He was forced to sell all his possessions and use up all his wealth to search for a cure. When his wife saw that he was impoverished, she left him. And when he could no longer provide for his children, they didn't want him anymore, either. After he recovered from the illness, he wandered from place to place, sifting through garbage in search of discarded items he could sell. But for some reason, not one house was open that day. The only place with an open door was the team's gathering place.

As Bambang and his teammates continued to get to know Cecep, they were eventually able to direct the conversation to Christ. As it turned out, Cecep's elementary school teacher was a Christian who liked to pray before starting class. "Even

---

[3] *"Assalamu alaikum"* is a common Muslim greeting meaning, "Peace be with you." The appropriate response is *"Wa alaikum assalaam"* which means, "And upon you be peace."

though I was a Muslim, I thought the teacher's prayer was beautiful," Cecep said. "Around fifth or sixth grade, I was actually interested in becoming a Christian. But when I graduated from elementary school, my parents enrolled me in a Muslim junior high school where I had daily instructions in Islam. I didn't like it so I dropped out and went to Jakarta to find work. It must have been God's plan, for I met many Christians in Jakarta." Bambang faithfully taught the gospel with Cecep, and Cecep responded by praying to receive Christ.

As a new believer, Cecep's greatest desire was to bring the gospel to his family, particularly to his children who had turned their backs on him. His eldest daughter, Leni, was married to an *ustad* and they had one child. News reached Cecep that his granddaughter was sick with a high fever. Leni and her husband had tried everything to find a cure for her. They had brought her to the local doctor, to the shaman, and to the other *ustad*[4] in the area in search of a remedy. But nothing they tried did any good.

Cecep decided to pay a visit to Leni's house. It happened to coincide with a ceremony led by the *ustad* from the local madrasah along with several of his students. When Cecep arrived, they were chanting Qur'anic verses over the child, but she was no better. The fever persisted, and the child was vomiting and had no appetite. Cecep immediately saw that her condition was most serious. So he asked his daughter, "Can I pray for her? Can I pray for my granddaughter?"

Leni, hesitating, said, "Let me check with the *ustad*."

---

[4] Muslim teachers often perform the role of traditional healer in the villages. For further discussion on this topic, it is recommended to read, *The Unseen Face of Islam* by Bill Musk, p. 115-121.

With the *ustad's* permission, Cecep went into the child's room. First he sang a praise chorus in his local Sundanese dialect. Then he took a glass of water, held it up, and prayed, "Jesus, two thousand years ago you turned water into wine. I am asking you to now turn water into medicine." He helped his granddaughter drink the water, and then he waited. It didn't take long. Ten minutes later, her fever broke and the child got up from her bed.

"The Christian prayer is amazing," the dumbfounded *ustad* said. "Even their songs are beautiful." News of the healing spread throughout the village.

Now that Leni and her husband had seen Christ's power first hand, they looked at Christianity with new eyes. Over the next two years, they met with Bambang and Cecep to study the Bible. Faith grew in their hearts, and they were baptized in 2010.

Bambang continued to seek out people whose hearts were open to Jesus Christ, and to share the gospel with them. Every day he prayed, "Lord, lead me to someone you have prepared to hear the good news today." One afternoon, as he went out to share the gospel, dark clouds gathered overhead. Before long, monsoon rain poured down in torrents. Thoroughly drenched, Bambang searched for a place to wait out the downpour. He spied a house nearby and dashed over to take shelter on the veranda. With rain thundering down, he introduced himself to Maryam, the woman who lived in the house. She said her husband Zubaidi was at work, but that Bambang should come again sometime and meet him.

Zubaidi had lived an unmotivated life. Every morning he awoke with his stomach aching from hunger. He would slip his sickle into his belt and go out to look for grass to cut for his goats to eat. Sometimes rich neighbors asked him to collect packs of cattle fodder for them. If no one gave him work, he would walk miles to some neighboring village in search of a day job.

Not long after Bambang met Maryam, he took his son Yosua and went to visit her and her husband. As soon as they arrived, Yosua began to cry. He begged his father to take him back home. The disturbance brought Zubaidi out to see what was going on. "I am so sorry," Bambang said. "My child Yosua started crying the moment we arrived at your house. He insists there is a scary looking old lady here."

Not the least bit surprised, Zubaidi said, "Oh, that's the spirit who watches over me. It's strange, though. When she saw you, she disappeared. You are not an average man." Before the spirit left, she had warned Zubaidi that if he became friends with Bambang she would leave for good. Even so, Zubaidi welcomed him to the house. Bambang came back again and again, and in time, Zubaidi came to know Christ.

Bambang prayed for Zubaidi, that he would break his relationship with the spirits and stop his occult practices. Zubaidi, who had learned the occult arts from a teacher in Banten, had supernatural abilities that allowed him to do such things as open a padlock without a key. He also kept magic amulets in the form of rings and stones.

By God's grace, Zubaidi was set free. After he was baptized, Bambang invited him to a retreat for Sundanese Christians. These retreats have greatly helped develop the fledgling faith of new believers who often live far away from other Christians. Some are the only Christians in their entire region. Isolated, they begin to feel inadequate and terribly insecure. Many simply keep quiet about their faith in Christ. Some are too afraid to even stand up for their legal rights.

The retreat's opening ceremony was truly moving. It started with dancers in blue flowing gowns who glided down the aisle to join up with the pastor and escort him into the meeting hall. As the pastor entered, carrying the Sundanese language Bible in a basket, Zubaidi started to weep. He saw, and really understood, that the gospel was not some foreign religion. It was for his people, too. By incorporating traditional arts and culture into their expression of Christianity, these retreats create a contextual Sundanese expression of Christianity. The retreat gave Zubaidi many opportunities to interact with other believers, and to hear how the Lord had worked in their lives. As Zubaidi joined with them, a change took place in him. We see that blessed change over and over as isolated believers, who come to the retreat feeling weak and insignificant, go back home with a courage and boldness they never thought possible.

But not everyone who came to the retreat was a Christian believer. Many Muslims also attended. They had already heard the gospel through the ministry of church planters, but they were not yet ready to believe. One of these was a lady who had recently finished her work contract as a maid in Saudi Arabia and returned home. The entire time she worked in Saudi Arabia, she sent her paycheck back to her daughter and son-in-law for safekeeping. But when she got home, she discovered that they had spent all her money. She had absolutely nothing to show for two years of hard work in a foreign land. Her heart was flush with bitterness towards her daughter and son-in-law when she met a SCF church planter. He encouraged her to attend the retreat. During a small group session, she met Zubaidi and several others. She was so moved by the lives of those Sundanese Christians that by the end of the retreat she had also put her faith in Christ. Filled with emotion, she said, "For the first time, I know what true love is."

Zubaidi returned home from the retreat filled with a sense of God's presence, and confident that He would use him in the days ahead. But already storm clouds were gathering on the horizon. The following day, Zubaidi went out to cut grass for his goats as usual. But when he returned home that afternoon, Pak RT[5] appeared at his house, along with Pak Haji, the head of the mosque. Pak RT said, "Assalamu alaikum."

"Wa alaikum assalaam," Zubaidi replied. "What brings you to my house? Usually you do not stop here."

At that moment, loudspeakers from a nearby mosque blasted out the call to prayer. Pak RT had to wait before he could answer. But Zubaidi could feel the tension and hostility in the air. His wife, old and frail, stood speechless beside him.

"I am just paying a friendly visit," Pak RT said politely. "As a community leader I should be out visiting the people of my neighborhood."

Zubaidi invited them to come in and sit down. Then he asked again, "What is it that has brought you to my house today?"

"Besides wanting to pay you a visit," Pak RT said, "there is a matter I wanted to ask you about."

"Certainly," Zubaidi said cautiously. "Go ahead"

---

[5] RT is the Indonesian abbreviation for *Rukun Tetangga* which is the sub-ward leader. The RT leader is the unpaid beginning of the chain of local officials overseeing a group of 10-20 households. Pak RT is the title for this local leader. Although they have very little legal power, an RT leader does have plenty of social influence.

"Well, before I do, I want to apologize for even needing to ask such a question. But many people in the neighborhood are saying things about you."

This surprised Zubaidi. "I am not a person of influence here. Why would they want to talk about me?"

"We have heard from a trustworthy source, someone close to you, that you have become a Christian." Pak RT's voice was no longer so cordial. "They say that you attended a special gathering for Sundanese people and were baptized there."

Zubaidi took a deep breath and calmly replied, "Thank you for telling me this. Since you already know about it, you have saved me the trouble of having to seek you out to report it to you. So what is the problem with my becoming a Christian?"

Pak Haji, who had so far listened in silence, spoke up. "Now, Zubaidi, take our advice. It's time to make an important decision. Renounce *that* faith and embrace Islam again. Do not be foolish, my friend. Throw away that garbage from the Christians. But if…"

"Wait a moment, Pak Haji," Zubaidi interrupted. "You are my best friend, but do not pressure me to change my mind. I have expressed my intention. I have made my decision. Why do you not listen to what I have to say?"

"What could you possibly have to say on this matter?" Pak RT snapped. He took a puff from his cheap cigarette and glared at Zubaidi with contempt.

"Friends," Zubaidi stated. "In the first place I didn't choose Jesus. Jesus chose me. I'm now His son. For the rest of my life, Jesus will carry me upon His shoulders. He leads me in fertile green pastures. I will follow my Good Shepherd with all my heart and with a clean conscience. I suggest that you repent of your sins and believe in Jesus, too, and you will also be saved."

To Zubaidi's Muslim guests, these words were like a resounding slap in the face. Zubaidi was a stocky man with a rough, unshaven face. He had never gotten a proper education. How had this simple neighbor of theirs become so eloquent a speaker? And how dare he challenge them!

Maryam sat stiffly beside her husband. Never before had she been subjected to an interrogation. She felt sick, but she couldn't move. A group of Muslim youths waited outside with sticks and machetes. What if her husband kept talking about faith in Jesus? What if the mob turned angry and burned down her house? Would they let Zubaidi walk away alive?

"Are you already baptized? Answer me honestly!" Pak Haji demanded.

"Yes, I am."

"How much did the infidels pay you? One million Rupiah? Three million Rupiah?"[6] Pak RT demanded.

"They paid me nothing. I didn't receive a single Rupiah. Who told you such lies? Does a man need millions if he already has wealth and abundance in Christ?"

Pak RT stared at Zubaidi, perplexed by his words. He had wealth? And abundance in Christ? Ridiculous! Anyone could see he was an extremely poor man. He demanded, "Zubaidi,

---

[6] It is a common assumption among Muslims that when someone leaves Islam it is because they are offered something such as money, a job, etc. Islam does not have the concept of a spiritual repentance.

what did the Christians give you as an incentive to convert? Tell me!"

Zubaidi was deeply offended by Pak RT's accusation, yet he took a deep breath and replied evenly. "You have it all wrong. When I was a Muslim you often came to me to ask for my help with our Islamic activities in the village. Now that I am a Christian, it is also the same. If I want to eat, I must work. With any extra, I give to help other Christians. No one has given me any money to convert. I became a Christian because I wanted to find salvation. While I was a Muslim, I often worried, 'Where will I go after I die?' I studied the Qur'an and I prayed at the mosque, but I got no answer to my question."

"So, you say that in Christianity there is salvation. Well, it is the same in Islam."

"Pak RT, I want to ask you. If God ended your life tonight, do you know where you would go?"

Shifting nervously in his chair, Pak RT answered, "That is none of our business. Only God knows such thing. What is important is that we follow his commands, do good works, and go on the Hajj Pilgrimage to Mecca if we have enough money."

"That's exactly my point! That is why I became a Christian. You are diligent in doing your prayers at the mosque and reciting the Qur'an but when you die you have no idea where you will go or what will happen to you. What about me? I don't pray much and I cannot recite many verses from the Qur'an. When I die, what hope is there for me?" Zubaidi was just warming up. "Even if you were to give me sacks full of money, I cannot deny Jesus, my Savior. Nor will I return to Islam. Jesus knows ...."

"Shut up, you liar!" Pak Haji blurted out. Blood rushed to his already red face. "I don't need more proof! I have heard enough from you. Zubaidi, you are no longer accepted among us. You will bathe together with devils in a fiery hell! You'll see!" Clenching his right hand, he turned to Pak RT and said, "When this perverted man dies, you are to waste no effort burying him!"

Even though this greatly distressed Zubaidi, he knew God was his protector. His favorite Bible passage flashed into his mind: *The LORD is my shepherd, I lack nothing. He makes me lie down in green pastures.* To his visitors he said, "If I die, just dump my dead body in the valley, or in the open sea. I don't care. My soul will have already gone to my Father's place."

As abruptly as they had come, Pak RT and Pak Haji left. Zubaidi and Maryam stood in silence. Zubaidi knew his wife was about to burst into tears, but before he could touch her arms, she slapped him on his left cheek. Zubaidi didn't move. Quietly he asked, "Why did you slap me? You have never done that before." Then he turned his right cheek toward her, squeezed his eyes closed, and waited for a second slap. But Maryam didn't slap him again. She covered her face and wept.

The following week, as Zubaidi walked back to his house after gathering grass for his goat, his neighbor yelled over to him, "Zubaidi, someone is looking for you."

Up ahead, Zubaidi could see a group of Muslim young men waiting on his veranda. He prayed, "Lord Jesus, I call to you. Help me Lord." When he reached the house, he greeted the young men. There were ten of them, and they had travelled from the West Java provincial capital of Bandung to see him. Zubaidi didn't have to ask why.

"Who forced you to convert to Christianity?" one of the young men asked. Just as he had done the previous week, Zubaidi said it was his personal decision, that he wanted assurance of salvation. No one paid him anything to convert.

Finally one of the Muslim youths spoke up. "Excuse me, Pak Ustad and my friends. I am not defending Zubaidi, but I have read their holy book, the Injil,[7] and it does say that Isa Al-Masih guarantees salvation for those who believe in him."

Pak Ustad grew quiet.

Taking advantage of the lull in the conversation, Zubaidi said, "I am surprised by all of this. In a nearby village there is an Ambonese Christian who converted to Islam. When that happened, none of the Christians were upset or caused a disturbance. Why is it that when a Muslim wants to become a Christian, you all get upset?"

"You are right," one of the young men said. "When a Muslim converts to Christianity everyone gets angry with him. It isn't fair. It seems like the Christians never act like that."

"Please, all that is important to me is that I can worship God in peace," Zubaidi said. "Do not forbid me to do that. If Pak RT or Pak Ustad needs my help for something, I am still willing to assist them."

That was the end of the intimidation. From that day on, Zubaidi worshiped God freely.

---

[7] Injil is the Arabic term for the gospel

CHAPTER 11

Weathering the Storm

The village elders that surrounded Anton had invited themselves into his house. "People in this village have become Christians! Who is responsible for that?" they demanded.

Apparently the conversions immediately led people to suspect that Anton, a 25-year-old church planter with SCF, was the source of it all. What he said mattered not. The village leaders had already decided to hold a kangaroo court at Anton's house. They shot question after question at him: How did he know certain people in the village? Why were those people now attending the house church? Had any of them been baptized? They fired their questions in rapid succession. Anton sat silently, praying to God in his heart for strength and the right words to say.

"Why don't you say something!" screamed an irate man.

Calmly Anton answered, "How can I say anything when you keep talking? If you will stop speaking and give me a chance, I will answer."

The men fell silent.

"I am a salesman,[1]" Anton said. "Every day I must go out and meet with many people. I don't only know the people you named. I know many others as well. Of course I have spoken at length with the people you mentioned. And, yes, I have invited them to stop over at my house, just as they have invited me to their houses. We have discussed many different topics. I do not deny it. One of those topics is religion. Now, if some of them choose to convert after hearing the teaching about salvation, that is not because of me. It is the Lord who has chosen them."

The village leaders could not refute Anton's answer, so they left his house and returned home. But they didn't go without a warning: "Stop speaking about Christ! That is an order." It was the beginning of April 2005.

The leaders came back a second time, but again they were unable to get to the bottom of the matter. So they returned a third time. And they ratcheted up the pressure by raising false accusations and slandering Anton. Thinking back on that day, he recalled, "I thought, if this is going to be my last day on earth, then I must be courageous."

And courageous he was. Even through the intense debate, in which Anton was verbally assaulted. Even when the village leaders demanded to know why he told the gospel to people of their village and made them into Christians. They brought up the case of Hussein, who was suffering from syphilis and could not walk upright because of the intense irritation to his genitals. Anton had seen the suffering man for himself, pus oozing from his infection. And he had shared the gospel with the man for

---

[1] The SCF church planters created secular identities for themselves so they could be accepted in Muslim areas. Their presence there as a Christian worker would have immediately closed whatever doors in the village that may have been open to them.

more than thirty minutes. Because Hussein demonstrated great faith, Anton laid hands on him and prayed for him. The following day, Hussein came to Anton's house walking upright. And now the village leaders wanted to make an issue of it!

"Who is Hussein?" Anton said as he began his defense. "He is a gang member. When Hussein was sick, no one in this village cared for him. They pushed him away. Not I. I came to him and prayed for him. But it was not because of me that he was helped. It was the Lord Jesus Christ who did this, in response to Hussein's faith in Him. Please, now, show me where I was wrong. I cared for someone who was sick and his condition improved, whereas you all let him suffer in that state."

Never wanting to miss an opportunity to testify about Christ, Anton continued. "Jesus is not just our source of help when we face problems in this world. He is also the only way of salvation for us after we die." The power of the Holy Spirit filled Anton and he continued to speak about salvation, while the village leaders sat in silence. In his mind, he thought, *Very soon, they may kill me.* Even so, he was convinced that the Holy Spirit was at work in the room, so he continued to share the gospel.

Finally the village leaders cut Anton off. With hardly a pause, they shot one accusation after another at him. The rest of this third trial was filled with slander and accusations aimed directly at him.

"We have records of all your visitors," one of the leaders stated. "You have had nine outsiders over to your house!"

"They once took someone from this village to Bandung and gave him a Bible!" another added. "If this isn't proselytizing, what is?"

"If I visit someone at their house, and that person welcomes me in, of course we are going to talk about something," Anton answered. "And I don't deny that when we sit and drink tea together, we discuss the topic of faith. What is the Christian faith like? What is the Muslim faith like? We discuss many things like this, and we have never had an argument over it. Now, if you are asking about my friends who have come to the village, I have no idea what they discussed when they visited people's homes in our village. You will have to ask them."

The leaders didn't like Anton's answer one bit. "But what about the book?" one demanded. "Why did they give you a Bible?"

"Look," Anton said. "If they did indeed give someone a Bible, please bring it here so I can see it for myself."

"We cannot do that. We have already burned it!"

Praise the Lord, Anton thought to himself. *They have no evidence.*

The village leaders thought Anton would be angry with them for lying about someone being given a Bible. Instead, he saw in it a way out of that line of questioning. Anton quoted from the Qur'an in Al Baqarah 2:191: *"If you have no evidence, then you are slandering me. 'Al-Fitnah [slander] is worse than killing.'"*[2]

---

[2] Quoted from the Quranic translation by T.U. Hilali-M. Khan

That line of questioning was getting the leaders nowhere. So the group's leader raised a different issue. "We know everyone in this area who has left Islam and became an apostate because of you and your friends. We know where they live, and we know everything about them."

"We have a fact finding team," another added.

Anton sighed. "If that is the case, then prove it to me. Bring them all here to meet with us."

"That would be impossible," said the leader. "They are spread out in different places. It would be too hard to bring them all here."

"We have only heard about these apostates," another said. "We ourselves have never met any of them."

Then Anton said, "That means you may be believing something that isn't true. You would do well to prove it first before you bring it up here."

When that didn't work, they took up a different tactic. They accused Anton of being a fugitive. "We know you used to rent a house ten kilometers from here. Pak RT in that village said you suddenly left after creating the same problem there that we have here."

Anton knew for certain that wasn't true. He had never lived anywhere in the province other than in the house he was currently renting. So he said, "If that's the case, bring Pak RT here. We can settle the matter right now."

The village leaders grew silent. Finally the leader admitted, "Well, we have heard rumors. . ."

"So it was all a lie," Anton said. "The fact is, you are slandering me!"

By the end of the two-hour long third trial, one of the elders in the village—an influential retired police officer—realized that Anton was indeed innocent. So during the fourth trial, he repeatedly opposed the others and took Anton's side. But the next day, he came to Anton with disappointing news: "The Islamic Defenders Front[3] did not accept the results of our interrogation of you. They said they will investigate, 'Anton down to his very roots.'"

Because the elder had defended Anton, people in the village had began to gossip about him. Alone with the elder, Anton said, "People are saying you expect me to marry your daughter in exchange for your support against these charges. I cannot imagine you would, since that would mean your daughter would have to become a Christian—an apostate in the eyes of the community."

The elder smiled. "That's nothing but a bunch of gossip. I really don't like the people of this village."

"They do seem like a bunch of troublemakers."

Anton knew that in the days to come, he would need as many people defending him as possible. How thankful he was that the Lord had softened the heart of this village elder.

The night before the fifth and final trial, Anton read through the book of Acts. After he read the account of the stoning of

---

[3] Indonesian: *Front Pembela Islam* or FPI is a hard-line Salafist group known for its raiding and intimidating places they deem un-Islamic, such as churches, bars, and gambling dens.

Stephen, he put his Bible down and prayed, "Lord, if I must die tomorrow, then I am ready. Receive my spirit into your presence."

In the presence of God! The very thought flooded Anton with a great sense of peace and joy. He considered the three possible outcomes: He could be set free, which would be a great miracle. He could be beaten and perhaps killed by a mob. He could be arrested and sent to prison. "Whatever happens tomorrow," Anton prayed, "I will praise You. And if I am released, I will never cease to testify of what an amazing God You are."

People gathered at Anton's house for the fifth trial. Outside, a crowd of machete wielding youth congregated in anticipation of a guilty verdict. They would be ready to execute swift justice. Everyone gasped when the city police chief arrived. Why would he come rather than the village level police officer who had been at the four previous trials?

The village leaders presented two witnesses—Syamsul and Rohanna, husband and wife, both illiterate farmers. "Are you Syamsul and Rohanna?" the trial leader asked. "Show us your identity cards."

"They expired long ago and we never got new ones," Syamsul said.

"Show us your baptism certificate," the leader demanded.

Anton did not like the rough way this couple was being treated, so he said. "They have been baptized. You can check with his older brother."

"What is his brother's name?" the police chief asked.

"Memet."

"Call Memet here immediately," ordered the police chief.

"That is not a problem, but it will take three hours because he lives far from here," Anton said.

The leaders murmured that they had no intention of waiting that that long, so the leader went back to questioning Syamsul and Rohanna. "Why did you become an apostate and follow Jesus Christ? Did Anton tell you to?"

"No, he did not," Syamsul said. "I decided on my own to believe in the Lord Jesus because He would save me."

How proud Anton was of Syamsul! Fearless in front of so many important people, and now he refused to deny his faith.

The police chief interrupted. "Anton, what is your occupation?"

But before Anton could answer, the village elder who had befriended him said, "He is a salesman."

Someone willing to speak up on his behalf! A miracle indeed! The police chief answered the next question, also in support of Anton. As it turned out, Anton hardly answered any questions during that fifth trial, because others continued to speak for him. So he spent his time praying.

Then the police chief brought up the matter of a poster placed at the ends of every street and foot path throughout the village that read:

"Beware of Christianization
Receive what they give you
But don't sell out your faith
ALLAHU AKBAR, ALLAHU AKBAR,
ALLAHU AKBAR"[4]

"Who is responsible for posting those signs?" the police chief demanded. But he didn't wait for an answer. "Such signs can only be posted with permission from the police. If you post them without our permission, you will be in big trouble. Don't you see that such a sign could lead people to think that the Christian minority is out to make trouble? That might well result in others punishing Christians by burning down their churches. And whose fault would that be? Yours! Because you put up those signs!"

Before Anton could open his mouth, the police chief roared, "Who told you to post these signs? Who is responsible?"

"It was the youth from the Islamic Defenders Front," someone in the crowd said. "They did it with the permission of Pak RW."[5]

The police chief turned to Pak RW. "Is it true? You did this?"

Pak RW blushed and stammered, "Well. . . yes. . . I did give permission. But I never read what was on the poster."

---

[4] Arabic meaning 'God is Great'

[5] RW is the Indonesian abbreviation for *Rukun Warga* which is the ward leader. The RW leader oversees 5-10 RTs. Pak RW is the respectful address for this local leader.

"All those posters must be removed!" the police chief ordered. A wave of panic and fear spread among the village leaders.

"I know of Anton's faith," the police chief continued. "Christians are commanded by their God to share their faith with others. Anton is only following that command. He is not wrong to do so. He is only in error if he *compels* someone to take on the Christian faith and become an apostate from Islam. I have not heard any proof that Anton has ever forced anyone to do so."

Anton gasped in amazement. The Lord was actually defending him via a Muslim police chief!

The leader of the trial announced his verdict: "We declare Anton not guilty of proselytizing." He glared at Anton and added, "But beware. If you convert anyone else in this area, I will burn you myself!"

Though painful, this trial had some positive effects. Believers in the region grew more confident and courageous, more ready to tell of their faith in Christ. Even Anton was able to defend the gospel in spite of the great pressure he was under. And all the Christians praised God for the way He protects His children.

After all Anton had been through, the leader of SCF told him to take some time to relax. But Anton would have none of it. He could no longer share his faith in the village, but there were many other places he could go and tell the good news.

For the next five months or so, a young man followed Anton everywhere he went to make certain he was not turning more Muslims away from Islam. Whenever he walked through the village, the youth would cry out after him, "Satan is passing by."

Anton just smiled. He knew the truth. The Lord Himself walked beside him.

CHAPTER 12

Clusters of Fruit

As Anton led the house church meeting, his Bible open on his lap, two men appeared at the door. It was Nabil, who served as the RW, and Pak Dukun.[1] Anton invited them in, then went right back to teaching from the Bible. Only this time he used a different theme – one he thought more appropriate for the two surprise visitors. Before they could address the matter that brought them to his house, they must first listen to Anton's teaching.

"Friends, I have a story for you entitled *The Eternal Hope In Heaven*." Anton told the story of creation, of the Fall, then of the prophecies about the coming Lamb of God who would take away the sins of the world. He told about Jesus' death and resurrection. Everyone listened with rapt attention. When he finished, he turned to Nabil and Pak Dukun and asked, "Would the two of you like to receive Jesus as your Savior and Lord?

---

[1] The Dukun is the village shaman who practices magic arts to assist people in overcoming their problems such as recovering from an illness, finding a job, etc. Pak Dukun is the polite way to address this person.

The One who died to redeem you from your sins and give you eternal life?"

The two men stared at him. After a long silence, Nabil asked, "Why hasn't anyone told me this before?"

So, he had been listening. Anton smiled.

"If someone had shared it with me earlier, I would have followed Jesus from my youth." Nabil was now 75 years old.

Anton looked up at Nabil and said, "I want to pray for the two of you." Then he turned to Pak Dukun. "Do you also want to accept Jesus as your Savior?"

Pak Dukun mumbled something to himself, as though he was repeating one of his incantations. Anton waited patiently for him to answer. After a long pause, Anton asked again, "Do you want to receive Jesus?"

"Yes," Pak Dukun replied. "Yes, I do believe."

So Anton led the two of them in prayer to receive the Lord.

More than a year passed before Anton was able to meet them again. But finally in 2008 he visited Nabil at his house. Praise the Lord, Nabil's faith was still strong, and he held firm to Jesus. After that, Anton went to Nabil's house once a week to disciple him. During one of their Bible studies, Anton asked, "Now that the Lord has saved you, how about your wife, your children, and your grandchildren?"

Nabil nodded. "Next week when you come over, I will make sure my entire family is here." He quickly added, "But do not tell them it was my idea."

"It wasn't your idea," Anton said. "It was Christ's."

Amina was the first in Nabil's extended family to believe. Before long, she was baptized. She attended a Sundanese retreat held by SCF, and she brought three other family members with her.

Because of her faith in Christ, Amina was soon hit with persecution. "Leave this place tonight," her neighbors threatened. "We have no Christians here; only Muslims. You must leave!" After her husband beat her severely, Anton moved Amina to another place. A week later, the situation in the village had cooled down enough that she dared to return home.

About a month after that, Amina's husband, Guntur, fell ill. His stomach was in knots. It caused him such pain that he couldn't walk upright. He had no idea what was wrong, though he suspected it might be typhoid fever.

"What can I do?" Guntar pleaded to Anton. "I am not at all well."

Anton said, "If you believe in Jesus, let's pray to Him and ask Him to heal you."

"Yes, yes," Guntur said eagerly. "I truly do believe."

Anton read from Matthew 8, the story of the Centurion who showed great faith. *"Go! Let it be done just as you believed it would,"* Jesus said to the Centurion. Anton placed his hands on Guntur and prayed for healing. He warned Guntur to stay away from spicy food, then he returned home. The following day, Guntur's illness was gone. Not long afterward, Anton baptized him. Now Nabil, Amina, Guntur, and one of Nabil's grandsons had all come to faith.

One night Nabil's wife had a dream about heaven and hell. That dream showed her that the Lord had also chosen her for salvation.

Nabil took on an ever increasingly important role. Whenever someone in the area wanted to harm the new believers, Nabil stepped forward to offer them his protection. The Word of God spread through his extended family— eighteen members, from four different families, all accepted Christ.

Once again, people in the village rose up against the Christians. They wanted to throw them all out. But the believers in Christ found strength as, one-by-one, others came to faith and stood alongside them.

When Nabil's grandson received the Lord, the boy's father, Asep, came to Anton's house armed with a machete. Anton was able to use the near-attack to further explain the gospel to Asep. And Asep listened. One thing that attracted him was the love and kindness of Christians. He saw it in the way Amina responded after Guntur beat her for following Christ. He was also attracted by the great power of Jesus. Guntur told him how he had prayed, and the Lord healed him. Asep liked this because he longed to also have mystical power. He had spent a great deal of time and money trying to obtain it. He even performed ceremonies in which he invited forty different spirits to inhabit his body.

"Your mystical practices are useless," Anton told Asep. "Replace your futile attempts with the true power of Jesus Christ. Only He has the authority to heal others." After a great deal of time, and many hours of discussion, Asep received the Lord.

Asep's job was dredging sand out of the river. Lifting that heavy wet sand from the river bed and up into a container was backbreaking work. One day, a friend of his had an extremely sore back, but since the man badly needed the money, he limped to the river intending to spend the day dredging sand. When Asep saw his friend's predicament, he told him, "If you want to be healed, you must believe in the Lord Jesus Christ. If you believe, then I will pray for you." The desperate man agreed. In front of the other workers, Asep raised his voice and prayed loudly. "Now walk over to that rock and you will be healed," Asep said. As his friend shuffled slowly towards the rock, he felt his back loosened up. Soon he felt so much better he was able to go back to work.

The Lord gave Asep the gift of praying for others. When a neighbor fell victim to demon possession, three days passed and no mystical practice was able to drive the spirit out. In desperation, the village turned to Asep for help. He told them that only Jesus Christ could drive the spirit out from the man. But the people begged, "Please, please help him!" So Asep prayed a simple prayer asking for Jesus' power to come down. Immediately the spirit left the man.

Both Asep and Amina were used greatly by the Lord. Yet as they grew in their faith, they became more and more aware of a problem: Asep had not dealt with his previous ties to mysticism. In one of their discipleship sessions, Anton discussed this with Asep. They agreed to set a time to ask the house church members to join them in prayer for him. Anton and the other SCF church planters prayed and fasted on Asep's behalf. Anton was well aware of the many magic amulets Asep used to gain mystical powers. He told Asep to list all of them on a sheet of paper. Asep did.

While the house church prayed, Asep's eyes turned red and his body began to shake uncontrollably. The leaders brought him to the pool they used for baptisms, but the spirits so intimidated him that he suddenly cried out, "I cannot go into that water!"

Anton and the others read Scripture to Asep. They told him he must be baptized as a sign of obedience to the Lord Jesus.

"But if I go into the water, I might die," the distraught man pleaded.

After more prayer and counsel from the Word of God, Asep finally rested in the Lord's protection. Before he entered the pool, his shoulders felt crushed with a heavy burden. But when he rose up out of the water, the burden was gone. Everyone who saw it knew for certain that the devil could no longer intimidate him. The spirits had been defeated. From that day on, Asep prayed diligently. He attended the house church, and ministered to others.

Anton's next task was to train Amina and Asep to take up the leadership of the house church in that village. Because they were so uneducated, they both felt terribly inadequate to lead others. Yet they worked diligently. They were willing to learn, and Anton was ready to teach.

CHAPTER 13

Scorching Heat

"We must go through many hardships to enter the kingdom of God." (Acts 14:22)

A red minivan filled with passengers cruised along on an all-night trip across the island of Java. Abdi sat with his family in the back seat. He looked down at his two-month-old daughter asleep in his arms and breathed a prayer of thanksgiving. God had allowed him to take his family to Central Java to spend Christmas with his parents. It was wonderful, but now he was eager to get home and prepare for another year of ministry in West Java among the Sundanese. Abdi's wife slept next to him, their three-year-old daughter sandwiched between them. Comfortable and blessed, Abdi drifted in and out of sleep.

Suddenly a passenger bus roared around another vehicle on the two lane road and slammed into the rear of the minivan. The driver lost control and swerved into the opposite lane. Fortunately, there was no on-coming traffic, but the minivan smashed into a telephone pole. Abdi's baby daughter flew from his arms and into the air. She hit the roof of the minivan before falling to the floor. The pole crashed down, crushing the minivan. Cries of agony cut through the air. Abdi's wife, her leg crushed between the seats, added her own screams of pain.

It was four in the morning when I received the call from Domu telling me Abdi had been in an accident. He and his family were at a government health clinic five hours away. I immediately called Abdi on his cellular phone, but when I asked how he was, all I heard was a woman screaming. It was New Year's Day, 2007. Immediately I drove out to the clinic to lend whatever assistance I could.

When I pulled into the clinic's parking lot, I noticed a lot of people milling around outside. I hurried past them and asked the nurse if I could see a patient named Abdi. While I waited for an answer, my ears rang with terrifying screams. The nurse pointed me in the direction of the howling. What I saw in the room was appalling. Abdi sat on a table holding his daughter. His face was battered and bloodied. He didn't say a word, but simply stared in a state of shock. His wife lay next to him writhing in pain from a compound fracture of her leg. Miraculously, neither of the little girls had been injured.

I called for the nurse and asked what pain medication Abdi's wife had received. The nurse said she'd had none at all. In Indonesia, no medicine is given until payment is received. Fortunately, I'd just been given a gift of a couple hundred dollars the night before so I had some cash on hand. With that, I purchased pain medicine which the nurse quickly administered. Government clinics are notorious for poor treatment, and Abdi's wife had suffered severe injuries. I knew her best chance for recovery would be in the city. I must take the family back with me. By folding up the back seat of my car,

I was able to make enough room for Abdi's wife to lie flat on a mattress I bought, and my makeshift ambulance departed on the five hour trip home. But Abdi had nowhere to sit. So for the entire trip, he stood up hunched over.

I remember thinking to myself, *This guy is incredible. In the middle of the night he is smashed around in a gruesome accident, has tried to care for his family while in a state of shock, and now he is going to ride hunched over for five hours. And not a word of complaint.* I shouldn't have been surprised. Church planters are amazing people. They have proven themselves willing to accept all kinds of difficulties and dangers for the sake of making Christ known among the Muslims. We have so much to learn from them. They are like Paul, who wrote, *"I have been constantly on the move. I have been in danger from rivers, in danger from bandits, in danger from my fellow Jews, in danger from Gentiles; in danger in the city, in danger in the country, in danger at sea; and in danger from false believers. I have labored and toiled and have often gone without sleep; I have known hunger and thirst and have often gone without food; I have been cold and naked."* (II Corinthians 11:26-27)

Over the next year, Abdi's wife needed several operations. And in the first weeks, Abdi took her back to the hospital every day. They took their three-year-old along with them, but the entire time, Domu and Tati cared for their baby. Yet sorrow filled Abdi. His wife and daughters should have died in that accident. He knew that. God had spared his daughters from any injury at all. He knew that, too. Even so, he struggled to make sense of what had happened.

One day, while he sat in the hospital room, Abdi and his wife talked through all that had happened the past few weeks.

In the end, they agreed: the Lord wanted them to renew their commitment to the ministry. Even so, for the time being, Abdi needed to cut back in order to care for his wife. That's how it had to be. Abdi prayed, "Lord, I will fulfill my responsibility to take care of my children during this recovery period. I only ask that you pay back this service to my family by bringing new souls to Christ."

And that is exactly what happened. Twelve people in his area followed the Lord in baptism.

One afternoon, Abdi was out walking with his daughter. As they made their way across the rice paddies, he came upon a woman sitting beneath a tree. "Good afternoon," she said politely. "Where are you off to today?"

"I decided to take my daughter out for a walk," Abdi said. "My wife is recovering from an accident and I wanted to give her a break."

The woman said her name was Lina. Abdi started to direct the conversation to the gospel, but he quickly sensed that she was not interested in talking about spiritual things. Still, Abdi visited her a couple more times. On one visit, Lina introduced him to her sister Meimunah. Meimunah had a completely different response. She told Abdi all about her life, her autistic child, and her husband who took a fourth wife when she was away working in another country. As the first wife, Meimunah was not allowed to be around other men, even though her husband didn't provide for any of her needs and only visited her once a month. Abdi listened carefully to all she said.

Before he left, Abdi prayed for Meimunah. "Hope in the Lord," he told her. "The Lord is alive and He comes near to those who call on him. I am a Christian and my Lord is Jesus Christ."

Every time he went to see Meimunah, she tearfully told more of her story. And Abdi shared more about Jesus—His death and His resurrection. In time, Meimunah accepted the Lord into her life. Immediately, her life changed. Although nothing had changed at home, she felt as though a burden had been lifted from her.

The next time Abdi came to Meimunah's house, he found her smiling. The tears were gone and in their place was the joy of knowing that the Lord was watching over her. Over the next few months, Meimunah gained back some of the weight she had lost. She laughed, and was able to talk about things other than her troubles.

Meimunah told Abdi that her hope for her old age was her son who was still studying in elementary school. The child's father had deserted him, and the boy suffered deep psychological scars from it. So Abdi spent a great deal of time with him. Once, while the boy was riding on the back of Abdi's motorcycle, he said, "My father never did this with me. He never did anything with me." Abdi couldn't miss the bitterness that had already taken root in the child's heart.

No one around Meimunah could miss the drastic change in her life. She began to attend the house church meetings, and within a year she was baptized. One afternoon, Meimunah's older brother caught up with Meimunah's husband. "Because you never come home and watch over your family, now your wife has become a Christian!" he scolded. The news infuriated Meimunah's husband. He rushed to her house, her brother right behind him. As soon as her husband saw her, he flew into a rage and started beating her. He threw her to the ground, and he and her brother kicked her until she lost consciousness.

While she was unconscious, the police came in response to a call by the village officials. They reprimanded her husband and made him promise not to do such a thing again. Her husband tried to argue that it was a family matter because it dealt with Meimunah's apostasy, but the police insisted it was domestic abuse. The Lord used the policemen to protect Meimunah from further harm.

Three hours later, Meimunah finally regained consciousness. Slowly, carefully, she tried to move her bruised and swollen left arm, but it was too painful. She looked straight at her husband and said, "If you want to kill me, go ahead. But I will never turn away from Christ."

Abdi and the other church planters had not been able to come to Meimunah's assistance because the police were there. It was her uncle, who was visiting from a village four hours away, who rose to her defense. He protected her, then brought her back to his village until she recovered from her wounds. As for Meimunah's brother, the police told him that because he had participated in the beatings, he must pay her medical bills.

Unfortunately this was not the only time Meimunah was persecuted for her faith. After she returned home, her brother came over and again beat her mercilessly. Even her grown daughter, Nani, turned on her. "I don't want to have a Christian mother!" she shouted. "Christians are infidels. I will never be willing to have a mother who's a Christian!" Nani and her husband so hated Meimunah that they moved out of the house.

Meimunah's younger brother knew she went to the house church meeting each week, so early one Sunday he came to her house, piled her clothes in her front yard, and set them on fire. If she had nothing to wear, he thought, she couldn't go to church. But when news of this reached the house church, people brought some of their own clothes for her. Meimunah told them, "No matter what challenges I face, I will not leave Christ."

Several months later, Meimunah's husband came to the house and smashed up her television set, her tape player, anything he could get his hands on. What he couldn't smash, he threw out the windows, shattering glass everywhere. Then he stormed out of the house. After Meimunah recovered from the shock, she cleaned up the house and covered the broken windows with pieces of plywood.

Early in January 2009, one of Nani's children fell ill. Meimunah went to visit her grandchild. With hatred written all over her face, Nani demanded, "How dare you come here! What do you want?"

Meimunah answered gently, "Only to see my sick grandchild." Then she asked, "May I pray for her healing?" Nani thought for a few moments, but finally agreed to allow her mother to pray.

Even though Meimunah was treated with such hatred, she continued to respond to her family with love and gentleness. Then in February 2009, Nani came to visit her mother. She said she was most eager to learn about Christianity. Meimunah asked in surprise, "What makes you want to do that?"

"I've been looking more closely at your life, and I saw how happy you are," Nani said. "In spite of the many problems you're dealing with. After all we've done to you. Still you respond to our hatred with love." Two weeks later, Nani made the decision to believe in Jesus. Meimunah's unfailing love turned Nani's hatred for Christ to love.

Meimunah's faith was tested for a fourth time when her husband came to her house with a samurai sword shouting that he was going to cut off her head. Meimunah fled in terror, but she tripped on a stone and fell to the ground. Her husband jumped on her. With his foot on her back, he raised the sword, ready to strike a blow. But before he could bring the sword down, his fifth grade son ran up and threw himself on top of his mother. They raised such a commotion that the village turned out to see what was happening. The villagers managed to calm down Meimunah's husband.

Not wanting to inflame the situation further, Meimunah sent a text message to Abdi and the other church planters telling them not to come to her house. Nor could Meimunah leave her house. Even so, the house church was determined to find a way to comfort her and stand beside her in her trials. They prayed about it and decided to send Tati to visit her. Another Sundanese woman wouldn't raise suspicion. Also, Tati was uniquely qualified since she had been beaten by her own husband for accepting the Lord. She was returning from the house church meeting when he surprised her on the road. In a fit of rage, he hit her, threw her to the ground, and stomped on her, leaving her face battered and bruised. Just as the house church had helped Tati through her crisis, the Lord now used Tati to come alongside Meimunah.

As the church had hoped, Tati's experience greatly encouraged and strengthened Meimunah. Tati connected with her heart-to-heart in a way that would not have been possible for anyone else. Meimunah learned so much from Tati's experience.

When Meimunah finally met up with Abdi, she asked him, "How much longer will I have to endure this?"

Abdi had no easy answer. "Be confident that this will also pass," he said. "If God allows it to happen to you, rejoice in knowing He considers you strong enough to endure under it. I am not sure I would be able to go through all you have suffered."

"If I am killed, I will be happier because I will go to heaven sooner," Meimunah said. "I will never reject the Lord, whatever they do to me."

It was Meimunah's younger brother who lived next door to her who administered the fifth round of beatings. The family turned to him because they had run out of ways to "persuade" Meimunah to change her mind. They had beaten her several times, smashed everything in her house, called her all sorts of unsavory names, and ostracized her from the family. Still she remained steadfast in her decision to worship Jesus.

Over a course of many weeks, an *ustad* had tried to convince Meimunah to return to Islam. But she refused each time. She said, "Whatever happens to me, I will always remain a Christian because Jesus saved me!"

The *ustad* schemed with Meimunah's younger brother to find a way to apply enough pressure to compel her to return to Islam. They came to her house one day and began beating her, saying, "You are so hard-headed! This is what you get for not wanting to be Muslim!"

To their surprise, Meimunah's face remained calm and peaceful, even during the violent beating. Over and over she told them, "Even though I must die, I will continue to follow Christ."

Finally Meimunah's brother realized that this was getting them nowhere. He asked her, "Why are you still following this Christ, even after you have been divorced, humiliated, and beaten?"

"Because Jesus saved me and gave me everlasting life in heaven after I die," Meimunah told her brother. "That is more important than this short life on earth?"

"Okay. Fine," her tormentors told her. "If that is how it will be, we will leave you to be a Christian. We will bother you no more."

CHAPTER 14

Weeding and Watering

In early 1999, Domu asked Satrio and Lina to lead a new team that would open the region of Ciharapan to the gospel[1]. After much prayer, they agreed. Six months later, SCF gathered together to commission the team. As the couple set out in a van filled with everything they owned, they struggled with their goodbyes—to their friends, to their first home, to their place of ministry in West Java. Even so, they eagerly anticipated the new work God had planned for them. As the van wound its way up the road and over the mountain to Ciharapan, they grew more and more excited.

Satrio and Lina's previous ministry experience helped then assimilate into their new community more quickly, and share the gospel more effectively. By Easter of the next year, they gathered interested people together to celebrate Christ's Resurrection. During that first year, seven people came to faith. But not everything came easily in Ciharapan. A reporter investigated one new believer and tried to get her to tell who was responsible for her conversion. The Holy Spirit gave her

---

[1] The other chapters of the book follow events in a chronological order. However, this chapter covers events from 1999-2010.

words to answer without endangering the others. Again and again, the church planting team faced intimidation. But every time they responded the same way—with prayer and fasting. Many times they spent the entire night asking God to intercede on behalf of His people. And God continued to add to His church. More church planters came to help, and the outreach in the greater Ciharapan region expanded even more quickly.

And upon completion of his training, SCF sent Yahya to Ciharapan in August 2004. Immediately he set out to build good relationships with his neighbors. This was especially important because few outsiders lived in the area. Yahya got involved in various community activities, such as soccer and ping pong competitions. This gave him wonderful opportunities to become involved in people's lives. He used his new relationships to share the gospel.

Sutrisno, one of Yahya's teammates, suggested, "This Christmas, how about if each of us invites neighbors to our house to share the story of the birth of Christ?"

Christmas always presented a special opportunity. Indonesians recognize six religions,[2] and each is allocated a national holiday. For Christians, the holiday is Christmas, since the birth of Christ is not offensive to Muslims. The Qur'an teaches that Jesus was born of a virgin, but denies that He was crucified and rose again. SCF church planters can invite their Muslim neighbors to their houses to join them in celebrating Christmas. Muslims come because they want to fulfill their social obligation of being neighborly. Christians do the same by attending village celebrations on Muslim holy days.

---

[2] The six religions are Islam, Protestantism, Catholicism, Buddhism, Hinduism, and Confucism.

Yahya enthusiastically agreed with Sutrisno idea. "My birthday is December 24. I can invite people to celebrate with me."

When Yahya told Pak RT about his plans, the leader offered, "Make up an invitation and I will distribute it."

"Should I follow any special format?" Yahya asked. He wanted to be certain he followed the village norms.

Pak RT said anything would be fine as long as both Yahya and Pak Ustad signed it.

"And the food?"

"It is better if you ask the women in the village to prepare the meal," Pak RT advised. "You are a Christian. If you prepare it, people may wonder if it was done according to the Islamic dietary laws. If they suspect the food is not *halal*,[3] they won't attend your celebration."

On December 24, People filled Yahya's house. "We are glad to have Yahya as part of our community," Pak RT said in his opening remarks. He officially welcomed Yahya to the village. Next Pak Ustad spoke, saying much the same. Things went smoothly—until the final speaker. Yahya had asked his teammate Sutrisno to speak on behalf of his family who could not be present because they lived far away on another island.

"We greatly appreciate the warm welcome you all have extended to Yahya for the past four months," Sutrisno began. "It is not easy to move to a new place far from home. On our

---

[3] Muslims have strict dietary laws similar to Judaism. Halal is the Arabic word to pronounce that a food has been prepared in accordance with these laws and is permissible to eat.

birthdays we especially remember our home. It makes us lonely. But today is not just Yahya's birthday, it is also the birthday of Jesus Christ. He left His home and came to live among us, just as Yahya has done."

The mood inside the house changed dramatically.

"Jesus chose not to stay in heaven, but instead was willing to humble Himself and take on human form," Sutrisno continued. A couple of people got up and left. One was the village police officer. Sutrisno ignored them. "I want to read the story of Jesus' birth from the gospel and from the Qur'an." When he finished reading, Sutrisno turned to Yahya and gave him this charge: "As the representative of your family, I advise you to rely always on Christ, as all of us here must learn to do."

The formal program finished, Yahya had the food brought out. He was presented with a conical shaped mountain of yellow rice to cut and hand out to the guests.

When the last visitors left, Yahya cleaned up the house and went to bed. The following morning he left for the island of Sumatra to spend the holidays with his parents.

Yahya returned on January 2. The afternoon of January 3, Pak RT came to his house and handed him a letter. Yahya opened it and read a detailed list of religious activities in which he had been involved. While Yahya was away, the village leaders had collected information about all his activities over the past four months. The letter concluded, "In relation to the event held on December 24 at your house, we request that Yahya appear before the village to give an account for the incident which has cause great unease among the people of this village." He was to be at the village office at nine the next morning. Yahya's mind raced: *Perhaps if I had not gone home*

*for Christmas, they would not have had time to investigate me
like this.*

Yahya arrived at the village office at five minutes before
nine. Many of the villagers were waiting. Finally at 10 o'clock,
the village leaders appeared, eager to get to the bottom of the
situation. Twenty-six people were prepared to speak with
Yahya. The village policeman was there, and so were the
village chief, RT, RW, and Niko, a representative from the
regional police station who came from the city to observe the
proceedings.

The village police officer began by reading the agenda for
the meeting. The first item was the accusations against Yahya.
"If you deny these accusations, this will only get worse," he
informed Yahya.

Help me Lord, Yahya prayed silently. *Whatever the
accusations, give me Your wisdom to answer each of the
charges.*

"On September 3, Yahya visited Parto's house and
discussed Christianity with him," the policeman began. Glaring
at Yahya, he demanded, "Is that correct?"

The crowd shouted, "Correct!"

One by one, the policeman read off twenty-two activities
considered illegal that Yahya had done in the past few months.
After each accusation, he repeated the question: "Is that
correct?" And each time the crowd responded, "Correct!"

Yahya didn't reply.

"Yahya, you have told all these people about Jesus and
prayed with them," the policeman accused.

This is all true, Yahya thought. *But how could they know everything?* Fear rose up in him.

After the trial had been going on for more than an hour, everyone was given something to drink. Everyone except Yahya.

"Accusation number 22," the policeman read. "They have gathered a small group of Sundanese people together, challenged them to receive Jesus, prayed with them, and said the 'Hail Mary.'"

The Hail Mary? That wasn't true! For Yahya, that accusation was like a divine intervention. His courage began to return.

Someone banged on the table and shouted, "We have heard enough! Yahya has been proselytizing, and he must be punished! What do you have to say for yourself, Yahya?"

"How many minutes am I allowed to speak?" Yahya asked.

"As many as you would like."

Yahya took a deep breath. "First allow me to greet you by saying *Assalamu alaikum.*

"*Wa alaikum assalaam,*" everyone replied in unison.

And to Niko, a Christian whom you have invited and I know well, I say peace be upon you."

"Concerning your accusations numbers 1 through 21, I do not deny them. But none of those activities was done through coercion. If you doubt me, bring the parties involved before us now and we will clarify the matter. I only invited them to various activities. No one was forced to come or to listen to what I had to say."

"Don't demand that we bring them here," they begged. "If they rise up and do something to you, we will not be responsible."

Yahya ignored their plea. "I am a Protestant. We do not say the 'Hail Mary.' That is a Catholic prayer. So your information is wrong. If you are wrong about that last accusation, you may also have wrong information about accusations 1 through 21."

Confusion broke out all around the room.

"We don't need to get confused here," Yahya said. "When someone asks me about my faith, if I didn't answer, how would that seem? So I answer them. After all, they asked the question. They want to know what the Bible teaches about the problems we face in this world."

Then Yahya turned the discussion around to where he could share the gospel with the village leaders seated before him. "In answer to their questions, I told them how God made man to be His highest creation. Everything was perfect and man lived in fellowship with God. God gave man free will to choose whether he wanted to obey God, and God placed him in the garden with the instructions, 'You may eat of any tree in the garden but you cannot eat from the Tree of the Knowledge of Good and Evil.' But Satan came and tempted man to eat the forbidden fruit." He looked at the leaders. "Isn't that correct?"

"Correct," they responded. Islam and Christianity share the story of the fall.

"This sin resulted in man becoming separated from God. The man and woman were ashamed because of their sin, and they hid from God in the garden." Starting with the fall, Yahya told of God's plan to restore man's relationship with Himself by sending Jesus to redeem us.

"All who believe in Jesus as their Savior and Lord—men and women, and even myself—we will have eternal life. That is what I told the people who asked. Nothing more. Is it wrong that I speak in this way?"

"No," they answered, "that is not wrong."

"Then why am I standing here before you today?" Yahya asked. "I have never forced anyone to become a Christian. All I have ever done was talk about Christ to those I have met."

"Niko hasn't spoken yet," the people said. "He is also a Christian."

"I am not that active in my faith since I only go to church on Christmas," Niko said, "but what Yahya told you is correct. He has not forced anyone to change their religion. If I was to forbid him from talking to me about Christ, then I would be sinning against the Lord Jesus."

Then the police officer who had called the meeting took charge. "That is enough for today," he said. "We are thankful for the Christians present in our village.[4] I only hope that what I heard today is true."

"No. I don't accept this!" Pak Ustad insisted. "Yahya cannot go around anymore talking to people about Jesus. I tell all the

---

[4] Actually Yahya was the only Christian from that village in attendance.

people here that they cannot receive Yahya as a visitor in their houses!"

With that, the trial was dismissed, and Yahya returned home. But over the next eight months, Yahya was not prevented from meeting people in the village and developing relationships with them. Even his relationship with the village policeman was restored. Some people in the village believed, but had not taken the step of baptism.

In the months following the trial, Yahya and Sutrisno met Mansyur in a nearby village famous for producing *kerupuk*, a shrimp cracker. Mansyur welcomed them into his home. During the next few weeks, as they continued to visit with him, they got to know him better. Mansyur was an *imam*[5] who diligently performed his five daily prayers (*salat*) and led the Friday noon day prayer service at the mosque. Although he was an extremely strong Muslim, Yahya and Sutrisno noticed something else about him. During one of their visits, a lady stopped and asked Mansyur to bless some water for her. She wanted to use it to get an answer to a struggle she was facing. Immediately the two Christians understood that Mansyur was not simply another *imam*. He was also a *dukun*, the village shaman.

Yahya and Sutrisno decided to spend a night in prayer for Mansyur. Two days later, they visited him and shared the gospel. The Lord touched Mansyur's heart.

---

[5] The *imam* is a Muslim religious leader whose activities include leading the Friday prayers at the mosque and instructing Muslims in their religious beliefs.

"Why is it that people come to you and ask you to bless them so they will become rich, yet you yourself are still so poor?" Yahya asked.

Mansyur understood that things were not right in his life. He agreed to study the Bible each week with Yahya and Sutrisno. The more they studied, the less frequently Mansyur attended the mosque on Friday to lead the prayers. Very quickly, the villagers became suspicious.

Then one day Yahya arrived at Mansyur's house to find both him and his only child sprawled across their beds. The Lord impressed on Yahya that Mansyur was ill because he worshipped other gods. Every day Yahya came to see Mansyur and nurse him and his daughter back to health. He also talked about the Lord's commandments concerning idol worship. Finally Mansyur admitted his mystical practices, and he received Jesus into his life.

Years later, looking back on his past life, Mansyur said, "Before I repented, I was a *dukun*. I did not know who the Lord Jesus was. I had visited all the holy places of Indonesia in search of mystical power: Cirebon, Gunung Kawi, Blitar, Madura and others. My desire for power was so extreme that I even stayed in the rainforest for forty days and forty nights, meditating and only eating leaves like a goat and drinking water.

"One of my amulets was a *keris*[6] knife. Every evening before *jumat kliwon*[7] at 11 p.m., the *keris* departed from where I placed it and did not return until 3 a.m. While the *keris* travelled to Cirebon, Gunung kawi and other places, I recited verses from the Qur'an. But this did not change my situation. I was still poor and owed a lot of money to the loan shark. My mystical powers helped many people. I was able to heal them, but I could not heal myself. I helped others overcome their financial problems, but I could not overcome my own. I had no peace within me until I found Jesus."

---

[6] A *keris* is a dagger with an asymmetrical blade and is considered to be a vessel for spirits.

[7] The Javanese calendar uses a five day week. *Kliwon* is the fifth and final day of the week. *Jumat* is Friday on a seven day a week modern calendar. When these two calendars overlapped concurrently, a certain Friday (*Jumat*) may also be a *Kliwon* day. This is known as *Jumat Kliwon*. That day holds special spiritual significance for Indonesian mystics.

One day, as Yahya drove along a deserted village road on his way to visit Mansyur, he repeatedly glanced at his rearview mirror. Another motorcycle seemed to be tailing him. When Yahya turned left, the bike behind him moved left also. When he sped up, so did the other motorbike. Frustrated, Yahya stopped his bike and parked it near a pedestrian crossing. He looked back, hoping that the one following him was an old friend. Thirty feet behind him, a man also stopped his bike, then lowered his left leg to the ground. Whoever it was wore sandals, and the hem of his long garment was lifted several inches above his ankle. Certainly this was not an old friend. Wisely Yahya cancelled his visit with Mansyur.

Yahya got off his motorbike and pretended to stretch and relax. Then, arms resting on his hips, he stole a look at the man. Ah, everything was fine. The man was only looking at a candy store on the other side of the street. *Just be a coincidence*, Yahya thought to himself.

But as Yahya rode his bike down a narrow path to a village, he noticed the same man behind him. His suspicions flooded back. Calmly, he slowed down. Without looking back, he approached a row of fruit sellers. In fluent Sundanese, he made great advantage of his bargaining skills. A half a pound of mangoes later, he drove straight back home.

Early the next morning, relieved that the previous day's stress was past, Yahya took his motorcycle out of the garage. Nothing serious had happened, so he figured all he needed to do was compensate for the lost hours by doubling his efforts. Wrong! The same mysterious man, riding the same motorbike, was again right behind him. Really irritated, Yahya pulled to a stop, but in the process he scraped the bottom of his bike on the edge of a long irrigation ditch.

What a waste! For two whole days he had achieved nothing. He plucked up a piece of grass and stuck it in his mouth. Chewing on it, he looked over at the spy who sat comfortably on the front veranda of a food stall, not ten yards away. The man looked clean. Young, too, not more than thirty years old. He wore a long white robe that flowed down below his knees, the type of clothing many Muslims wore for Friday gatherings in mosques. *He's probably from a hard line Salafist group determined to keep me from telling the gospel*, Yahya thought. Most likely the man was recording the names and addresses of everyone Yahya visited.

For an entire week the man shadowed Yahya, who found the whole thing extremely frustrating. Yahya continued to play hide and seek with him. Still, he did manage to secretly meet Sutrisno one night at midnight. Sutrisno gave him practical advice as to how he should respond to the situation. To protect the members of house churches, the ministry temporarily cancelled all their activities in six different locations.

After the situation settled down, Yahya again met with Mansyur and continued to disciple him. One night he and a friend went to Mansyur house to invite him to the Sundanese retreat. But Mansyur had a visitor, and since Yahya didn't want to risk raising suspicion, he and his friend pretended to be visiting Mansyur the *dukun* to ask for help with a problem. Mansyur told Yahya to wait in his room while he finished with the visitor. But when Yahya entered the room, he saw a shocking sight. Amulets lay strewn across the table – stones, *keris*, incantations, Arabic writing, Javanese writings, a snake statue and … the Bible Yahya had given him! It was covered in powder from some mystic ritual. With tears in his eyes, Yahya picked up the Bible and, with the bottom of his shirt, carefully cleaned it.

When Mansyur finished with his guest, he went the room where the two were waiting. Yahya looked at him with great sadness. "I came here to tell you something, but when I saw the Bible among these amulets, it made me too sad. I know it is a book that can be burned or stepped on, but most of all it is a Bible filled with wonderful truths."

Yahya's friend, who was well-versed in Indonesian mysticism, asked, "Mansyur, do you think that all those teachers are good? I have a teacher who is much greater than all of them put together."

Mansyur's eyes grew wider when he heard this.

"My teacher is the Lord Jesus Christ."

After much discussion, Yahya and his friend finally convinced Mansyur that he could no longer say he believed in Christ and at the same time hold on to his mystical practices. As a sign of his commitment to Christ, Mansyur took the *keris* from the table and handed it to Yahya. "I want you to take this away from my house," he said. "I got it from Cirebon. When you are taking it away, you must remember something. You cannot look back until after you have taken seven steps."

"God cannot be treated like that!" Yahya's friend said. "He is more powerful than your *keris*."

So Mansyur gave every one of his amulets to Yahya. Before he and his friend left, they prayed for Mansyur, asking the Lord to give him peace and rid him of every influence from evil spirits in his life. As for the amulets, they were all destroyed during SCF's prayer meeting for Mansyur.

It was many months before Mansyur was totally free from the evil spirits. During two other prayer sessions, he described other mystical practices besides the amulets. He had several diamond *susuk*[8] in his face. A *dukun* had implanted them to make Mansyur more handsome, and also to protect him from injury. Still, Mansyur's relationship to the spirit world showed itself in his wily actions. He constantly stirred up trouble for the church planters. But through prayer, he was finally set free. And it made a noticeable change in him. His emotions became more stable, and he was able to hold down a steady job.

It was not easy for Mansyur, but it was not easy for Yahya, either. "It felt like we were using more energy for this one man than if we had been shepherding 1,000 others," he confided.

We could really see the change in Manysur when he began to share the good news of Christ with his family and friends. He was often asked to give a massage to a person who was hurting. As he massaged, the person inevitably complained about the pain: "Ouch. That's the spot!" That was Mansyur's cue. "That pain is nothing compared to the pain experienced by Jesus," he would say. When the person asked who Jesus was and why He experienced such great suffering—and they almost always asked—Mansyur dove right in with the gospel. He also sold household items door to door, a job he saw as yet another means of evangelism. People liked Manysur. They liked to buy from him, too, because of his pleasant attitude towards them. Whenever someone said as much to him, Mansyur would reply, "The one who is good and filled with compassion is Jesus. As His follower, I must pursue His example and exhibit His qualities."

---

[8] A *susuk* is a needle embedded in the skin as a talisman.

Three in Manysur's village responded to the gospel. Two more wanted to believe, but problems arose before he could lead them to faith. The village discovered the Christian teachings when the men and women returned home from a Christmas celebration at the house church. Village leaders decided to pressure Mansyur through his wife's extended family. They insisted that he divorce his wife and leave the village. Pak *ustad*—the Muslim teacher of his village—and another village leader who had lost the election for RW to Mansyur, led the backlash against him. Both men harbored ill will towards him, and Mansyur's Christian faith gave them an excuse to get him out of the way. Under pressure, Mansyur lied to them. He claimed that he had been a Christian from the time he was just a child. In fact, as a young boy he did work for a Christian family, but he knew very little about their faith. The only thing he remembered was a single praise chorus.

Mansyer's in-laws were very much opposed to Christ, but they didn't want him expelled from the village. He was a good man. And he was providing for his wife and daughter, as well as for them. But when he lied about being a Christian since childhood, the villagers felt deceived. Hadn't he claimed to be a Muslim when he married? His lie also greatly upset his parents-in-law.

The village leaders reacted by writing a letter—which villagers signed—ordering Mansyur to leave their village. Then they summoned him to the village office for questioning. Confused, he wondered, *If this is about my problem with my in-laws, why do I need to be questioned at the village office?*

The meeting was set for 1:30 p.m., right after Friday prayers at the mosque. The situation in the village was reaching the boiling point. Both Mansyur and Yahya felt that it would not be wise for Mansyur to attend. They feared that the mob would turn against Mansyur even before the meeting began. So Mansyur stayed away. Yahya, however, donned a motorcycle helmet that covered his face and managed to get near the village office without being recognized. Outside, a large crowd gathered to await Mansyur's arrival. When he didn't show up, they set out to look for him. But Mansyur was nowhere to be found.

On Yahya's advice, Mansyur had moved to a different safe location where he could lay low during the meeting and for a few days afterward. When everyone cooled down, he went back home, and for the next two weeks, things were quiet. But then one night, several of the village youth threw stones at his house. The next day, Mansyur moved his family to Yahya's house until he could find a house to rent in another village.

After a couple of months, the whole issue faded away. Mansyur still goes back to his wife's village to sell household items. And many people in the village ask him what problem forced him and his family to leave. In their minds, people are only expelled from the village if they are criminals, such as drunks or adulterers or thieves. They cannot understand why a good man such as Mansyur would be expelled. His answer is simple. "I was run out of the village because of my faith in Jesus Christ."

Mansyur continues to visit those he led to the Lord. In spite of his problems, they have remained firm in their faith. In fact, when Mansyur moved away from the village, two of the believers wanted to come with him. "Even if we have to live in a bamboo hut, we want to follow you so you can teach us the Bible," they implored. But Mansyur told them not to worry. He was committed to visiting them regularly, and to teaching them.

During one session, a believer confided, "I'm afraid to share my faith with others here. I fear that I will be expelled from the village like you were."

"We have Jesus in our lives, so we do not need to be afraid," Mansyur said. "Look at my life now. I am still alive, aren't I? Remember, many young men came to my house one night and threw stones at it. But we are under the Lord's protection. We do not need to be afraid."

Mansyur's wife chose to remain with him rather than to follow her family's advice and divorce him. Now his wife's father has started to attend the house church. But because of the *ustad's* influence in the village, his wife's mother still will not attend.

As Yahya watched Mansyur and his ministry, he knew for certain the Lord had raised him up to bring the gospel to the Ciharapan region. So Yahya looked for other unevangelized areas in West Java. When he selected a new location, he called Mansyur to him and said, "I want you to take over for me here. As long as the door stays open, we need to tell people about Christ."

As Yahya's departure drew near, Mansyur came to his house every day and watched him pack up his things. Many times, Mansyur broke down in tears.

"Don't cry," Yahya told him. "I would be filled with sorrow too if it wasn't for your faith in Christ. May the Lord use you to bring many people to Himself."

CHAPTER 15

Birds in the Branches

Among the 400 Indonesians worshipping God at the church service I attended on my very first day in the country was Rudy Hartono, a famous badminton player. That was before I knew how crazy Indonesians are for badminton. In Barcelona, 1992—the first year the game was played in the Olympics—Indonesia won all five gold medals. Christians, although they are but a small minority of Indonesia's population, do have influence in the country.

And certainly the gospel is bearing fruit among the Sundanese people. The question is, what kind of fruit? We cannot be satisfied with seedless grapes. God's desire is for fruit with hearty seeds ready to sprout and grow into healthy new trees that will produce still more crops for the harvest.

The gospel is not only productive, it is also reproductive. And that is the most encouraging thing about our work. No longer are we merely laboring to start a church. Muslims are already putting their faith in Christ and being baptized. Now it is time to reproduce.

The Sundanese church of today fits the category of "the least of these." It has few resources, little education, and a slim slice of opportunities. Yet the Lord is using its believers to produce new seeds that will grow into strong, new trees. Mansyur, Memet, Amina, Saladin, Meimunah, and others like them will raise up the next generation of Sundanese Christ followers. These faithful believers actively share Christ with the people around them and lead them to faith. And their testimony is not only spiritual. They are actual witnesses to lives changed by the gospel. Memet, once an illiterate shaman (*dukun*), can now read and write. Through Meimunah, an autistic child moves forward surrounded by hope. Saladin provides for his family through his prospering business. People look at these Christians and see that the Lord does indeed bless those who "seek first the kingdom of God" (Matthew 6:25-34). They watch these believers commit their ways to the Lord and see the many ways in which they experience His promises.

It's not enough for the SCF church planters to simply introduce a Sundanese person to Christ and then move on to the next person. Discipling the new believers means addressing each area of their lives so that they grow and become more like Christ. The Sundanese community is watching to see what impact the gospel has on a new Christians' life—marriage, livelihood, health. . . every area. Tati is a good example. When her husband abandoned her, the Sundanese Christian Fellowship gave her money to buy a washing machine. Now she runs a business washing clothes for people in her neighborhood. And the community has taken notice. They see that she is alone, but the church did not desert her. Tati has been able to overcome both her marriage problems and economic hardship because of the gospel.

Cakra, a widower who lives with his daughter Bunga, is another example. Because he had to be both father and mother to his child, Cakra worked extremely long hours to provide for her needs. His first concern was to see that she got an education so she could have a better life than he was living. In his struggle to save money to pay her school fees, he skipped meals. But constant hunger and growing stress crippled him. His ulcer flared up so badly that he could no longer work. As Cakra's physical health declined, his great hope for Bunga faded into impossibility. Soon the girl had to spend her days caring for her bedridden father. She fell so far behind her class that she had to drop out of school.

Poverty had caught Cakra in its vicious cycle. He couldn't work because he was sick, which meant he had no money to go to the doctor and get a cure, which meant he couldn't work. Cakra had no idea how to break out of the cycle. When SCF church planters came to visit him, they took one look at his terrible condition and their hearts broke. Weak and pale, he lay all day long on his bed in a dark room. The church planters found no food in the house. They immediately took him to the clinic for medical treatment, then they hurried home to make food for him and to pray for him and his daughter. Three days later, they again visited Cakra. What a change! He was well, with a smile on his face. The workers continued to visit, and each time they explained more of the gospel. In time, both Cakra and Bunga put their faith in Christ.

It distressed the church planters to see that Bunga wasn't in school. She was obviously very intelligent. With funds made available through Partners International's Sponsor-A-Child program, they were able to provide enough financial assistance so that she could enroll for the upcoming school year. She was so excited to continue her studies that she didn't mind having to repeat a grade. That scholarship set her on track to graduate from high school. "I have seen for myself that the scholarship provided by Sponsor-A-Child has been a tremendous blessing in the lives of many children like Bunga," the SCF church planter said. "Bunga is such an intelligent child with good grades in school. It's a shame that people like her need to drop out of school because of financial problems. Praise God that we could help."

The future of the Sundanese church is in the hands of the young people. The current generation might not have had much in terms of opportunity or resources, but because of them, the seeds have been planted. Their work and growth will allow the next generation to grow up with unlimited possibilities. Because of the bridge these first believers built, the young people have the potential to fulfill the Great Commission among the Sundanese people.

For years we have been unable to minister to Muslim children in spite of their openness to the gospel because of the society's sensitivity to such Christian activities. Christians who have reached out to Muslim children have been jailed for disturbing the peace. But now, a new opportunity has opened up. As we have reached many adults with the gospel and they are now following Jesus, we are able to gather their children together and minister to them. Children who know Jesus at an early age will be able to impact their surroundings for years to come.

The first Bible Camp that SCF held for Sundanese youth was centered around the theme: Isa Al-Masih (Jesus Christ): The Way, The Truth and The Life. The camp's focus was explaining the gospel so the youth might respond to it and also equipping them to share that gospel with their Muslim friends and extended family members after they return to their villages. For many, the weeklong camp was the first time they were away from home for so long. Over the week, a sense of trust and family was created. This resulted in many of the youth opening up about their life's struggles.

Budi was experiencing the typical problems faced by so many in the teenage years. His parents did not understand him and were having difficulty in this transition time in their relationship. Regrettably Budi fell into the wrong crowd. He joined a gang and was involved in many sinful activities. Starting from the time he arrived at the camp, it was evident that he was a loner, keeping his distance from others. But by the second day, his attitude changed remarkably. After breakfast he grabbed a nearby guitar and began leading several of the youth in singing praise songs. By the end of the week, he was standing in front leading a vocal group. God so touched his life that he turned around 180 degrees.

What a joy it was to see the youth build one another up and strengthen each other for the future. On the last night of the camp, the youth came forward to commit their lives to the Lord. They were challenged to hold fast to their faith after they returned home from the camp. Their tears were evidence of their commitment to face their challenges as Christians in a Muslim village. They rose to their feet together and sang, "We Are More Than Conquerors." Thousands of Sundanese Muslims have turned to Christ with only few of us few at work. Imagine how that will multiply many time over when these young men and women, passionate about Christ and about their own people, go to work!

In addition to evangelism and church planting, the Sundanese Christian Fellowship has expanded its work to bring gospel impact to all facets of the culture and community. In reformed theology, this would be known as the "cultural mandate." The gospel must affect change in the arts, politics, education, health, economy, and every other part of society. For too long, these areas have been influenced by Islam. We must show the power in that truth of the gospel.

A major area of concern is education. Although public school is "free" in Indonesia, parents are burdened with many charges. They must pay entrance fees, buy books and uniforms and meals, pay for transportation, and handle a myriad of other expenses the school bills to them. The burden on families who live from day to day or harvest to harvest is overwhelming. Many children drop out before sixth grade. Yet without an education, children don't have much of a future. Without good education, Christian children will not have much an opportunity to impact their society.

In Indonesia, children are required to attend religion classes once a week, even in public schools. Since villages are usually 100 percent Muslim, the only religion classes offered are Islam. Children who have come to Christ no longer want to attend these classes. But to refuse is to publicly declare their faith in Christ. This opens them up to mocking and ridicule from other children. The principal calls their parents to the school and rebukes them for allowing their children to become Christians. It is yet another example of the built-in challenges that face those who come to faith in a Muslim society.

Amina's son, Kurnia, experienced this firsthand. Amina, a housewife and her husband Guntur, who worked as a day laborer in construction, had been active in the house church since their conversion. They also ministered to others. After they were baptized in 2007, their two children accepted their parents' faith. Young Kurnia always attended Sunday school at the house church. He asked his mother when he could be baptized. Amina told him, "Once you study more about the Christian faith and are a little older you can be baptized just like we were."

Early in 2010, Kurnia was enrolled in the Sponsor-A-Child program. He absolutely loved school, did well in his studies, and was an all-around good child. It was his dream to go to a Christian high school in the city. But first he needed to get his diploma from the Muslim principal of his middle school. Withholding diplomas in order to get more money from the family is a common practice. When Amina met with the principal to ask for her son's diploma, he asked, "Where does Kurnia plan on attending school next year?" Amina answered that he would be going to high school in the city. The principal huffed, "Oh, you must be sending him to a Christian school. Well, we have decided to enroll him in the public high school here in this village."

Amina had the sad task of telling Kurnia the principal's decision. There was nothing they could do about it. The principal was determined to keep the boy from attending a Christian school in the hope that he would return to the Islamic faith. Even though he was denied the opportunity to attend a Christian high school, and the better education it offered, Kurnia could still join the youth discipleship program. By gathering the young people together in such a way, the Sundanese Christian Fellowship hopes they will grow in their faith during their crucial high school years. They can even be salt and light in their villages.

As for Kurnia, he wants to serve the Lord when he is older. He is so impressed by the role Anton played in bringing the gospel to his village. Kurnia feels called to continue that mission by taking the gospel to others who have yet to hear about Christ. His parents rejoice at the path their son chose, and they plan to enroll him in Bible school after he completes high school.

Most of the work successfully done with the Sundanese has been among the lower class and those marginally employed. In Indonesian society, these are people of low status who have little influence. As long as the gospel is confined to them, it will be difficult to see meaningful movement.

During the first three centuries after Christ's resurrection, the gospel grew rapidly among the slave class of the Roman Empire. But eventually it made the jump from slaves to the citizens and aristocracy. But it wasn't until the Emperor Constantine followed Christ that persecution against the Church finally abated. With this history in mind, SCF sees young people who have the greatest potential as their main investment for the future. The goal is to raise up a generation of Christian nurses, police chiefs, judges, teachers, and businessmen who will return to their villages with the higher status that education and professionalism bring. As they perform their jobs with excellence, they will have a strong platform from which to share Christ. To this end, SCF has established a special program for promising youths. Those who are committed to Christ and show academic potential are brought to the city to study. Although the results are a generation away, SCF trusts in the promise of Galatians 6:9— *"Let us not become weary in doing good, for at the proper time we will reap a harvest if we do not give up."*

SCF's vision is to raise up a whole generation of well-disciplined, intelligent leaders who will work in all levels of village leadership. As they do so, this next generation will bring Christian values to their various spheres of influence. They will also strive to bring the gospel and Christ from the margins of Sundanese society into the mainstream.

Bakri was the first young person brought into this program. His parents became Christians and were baptized in 2005, the first Christians in their extended family. Although Bakri, who was in sixth grade, followed his parents' faith, he didn't really understand what it meant to be a Christian. His parents were quite limited in their ability to lead their family in their new faith.

The family had struggles, and in time, the parents divorced. This led to many problems for Bakri and his siblings. God strengthened Bakri's mother so that she remained steadfast as she raised her children alone. Even so, Bakri suffered during his early teenage years from not having a father. He grew cynical and skeptical towards others. One by one, his friends deserted him. With his life at a crossroad, he had no idea how to move forward. Looking back on that time, Bakri recalls, "God used that difficult period in my life to fulfill His plan for me. I felt God touch my soul through His Holy Spirit. Since that time, heavenly joy flowed through me. There was a change in my life. I felt a joy like I had never felt before. When I entered ninth grade, I committed myself totally to the Lord. I repented, and told God I would follow Him. My sins were forgiven and I was saved by His grace. I knew my life was valuable in God's sight."

Bakri realized that the Lord knew what he was experiencing. During his period of loneliness, God provided him with a gracious friend, and they developed a warm relationship. His friend encouraged Bakri to study diligently and to excel in school. When Bakri heard about the opportunity SCF was offering to study in the city, his friend suggested that he apply. It was a unique opportunity because the high schools in the city were much better than the one in Bakri's village. But no one in his village could go to the city high school. Not only was it more expensive, but such schools had a more rigorous academic standard. It was very difficult for students from the village to qualify.

"I didn't want to waste the opportunity," Bakri says. "I was entering the tenth grade, and I told my mother I was going to apply for a scholarship." He finished the written application, then he took the written test followed by a second round of written tests, and finally a personal interview. "I prayed and committed the results to the Lord. I was ready to accept, whatever the decision."

When the test results were announced, Bakri had passed. He was the first one accepted into the program. How did he feel about such an accomplishment? He said, "I hope I will be successful and give an example of godly character, good grades, and mature spirituality to those following after me."

In addition to regular school work, students in the program are part of a one-on-one discipleship program, and members of a youth group for Sundanese teenagers. They also help in SCF's community development work. Bakri is especially grateful that he can live with a Christian family that truly cares about him. Being surrounded by a strong Christian community has greatly impacted both his life and his character. "The Lord has brought me this far," he says. "I never imagined that this would have been His plan for my life."

Not that everything has gone smoothly for Bakri. In his second year of high school, he struggled in some of his classes. But he accepted it as part of God's processing of him. His second semester was particularly difficult. He failed to get good grades in physics and chemistry. "I felt guilty for not doing better in school," he says. "But my feeling of guilt did not cause me to give up. I applied myself even more diligently to my studies and now, praise God, I have the help of a tutor to help me in my science class." His favorite class is biology. He hopes to graduate from the university with a degree in nutrition. This is an important area, particularly in many villages of West Java where so many struggle with malnutrition. For his post graduate studies, he wants to attend a local seminary. That would allow him to develop a balanced approach to his academic path and his spiritual walk. When he finishes his studies, Bakri looks forward to serving the Lord. "I hope God will use me to be His instrument and blessing to the Sundanese people. May His name be glorified in my life."

Bakri is a young man who shows maturity beyond his years. He is growing in his faith through daily devotions as well as though his weekly discipleship meetings. He shares what he learns from the Bible teaching with other young believers in the house church.

The gospel message is good news indeed. Not only does it bring man to heaven, but it brings heaven down to man. As it is applied to lives in the various frameworks of Sundanese society, the fullness of God's redemptive plan will continue to be revealed. We can echo the words of Matthew 6: 10—*"Your kingdom come, your will be done, on earth as it is in heaven."*

We thank God for what he had done! And we praise Him for the exciting things just around the corner!

CHAPTER 16

Lessons from the Mustard Tree

In this book, we have seen how the story of God's work through the Sundanese Christian Fellowship has unfolded over twenty years. The Lord has done amazing things through faithful servants, and the gospel message has gone forward among the Sundanese people. From among many millions of Sundanese Muslims, several thousand have put their faith in Christ. Some of these faced great hardships, others did not. But all have one thing in common: Each one has been brought out of darkness and into the light. Each one has found true life in Christ and security for all eternity.

Being a part of a pioneer work among an unreached people group has taught me some important lessons.

Lesson #1: Calling is vitally important.

Without being sure of God's calling, I would have left Indonesia after twelve months. At the end of my first year, I was discouraged and felt totally alone. But God clearly reminded me that He had called me there and He had not yet told me to leave. Because of this clear calling, I stayed and the

Sundanese Christian Fellowship continued. So, how does one know he or she is called by God to a particular ministry? This is something with which every servant of God must wrestle. On many occasions, I've heard Domu say, "Many servants of God want to decide for themselves where they want to serve rather than allow God to decide for them." Our responsibility is to wait for God to call us to the place He has chosen to use us, and then to obediently go. The difference between those who last in the ministry and those who give up is often the clear discernment of one's calling. When things get tough and discouragement sets in, calling is what will keep you in the ministry.

Lesson #2: Hard does not mean impossible.

Pioneer church planting is probably the hardest ministry in the world. And church planting among Muslims is ten times harder! But hard doesn't mean impossible. The stories in this book represent but a small taste of what God is doing to draw Muslims to Himself. While it will take much faith and perseverance to succeed in this ministry, we can do it if we have the confidence that He is working and that His gospel will bear much fruit. There is no secret key to reaching people with the gospel. It takes much prayer and much evangelism – two things that seem to be lacking in the western Church today, I might add. Hard things can be done for God in the most difficult of places if we believe Him fully and are willing to pay the price to be faithful to our calling. The Apostle Paul tells us to *"Always give yourselves fully to the work of the Lord, because you know that your labor in the Lord is not in vain."* (I Corinthians 15:58) What great challenges is the Church facing today? Not a one that the power of the gospel and the kingdom of God cannot overcome. God invites us to join Him in this endeavor. Believe Him and His Word. Serve Him diligently, faithfully, and with great perseverance. He will work through you. You can be confident of that.

Lesson #3: Successful ministries are not about one person.

Most missionary stories are about a special person God raised up for a specific time in history. William Carey was one of these, and Hudson Taylor, Adoniram Judson, and many others. But SCF's story is different. It's about many people— average folks who took the gifts and energy the Lord gave them and used them for His purpose. It is a story of many people doing a lot of little things, each one fulfilling the part the Lord assigned to him or her. The Kingdom of God is that kind of story. It is a boy with five loaves and two fish. It is a man with a donkey the Lord wants to borrow. Too often we think that if we are not "spiritual giants," we cannot do anything important for God. That's not so. Each of us has been placed in a specific place at this precise moment of history for a reason. And each of us has been given the gifts and skills we need to perform the role God has assigned us in the building of His kingdom. As you reflect back on this book, here is something to consider: If a bunch of normal Christians could accomplish so much among the Muslim Sundanese, imagine what you can do if you give all you have and are to the Lord. This is the time the Church needs to rise to the challenge of our day. What gifts and abilities do you have? Give them to the Lord!

Lesson #4: We have one adversary, and it is not Islam.

Some might read the accounts in this book and conclude that Islam is the adversary. That couldn't be further from the truth. The frequent reports of Christians persecuted in Muslim lands, and the media's portrayal of Islam, reinforce the feeling of enmity and incite fear in us. Even influential politicians cite radical Islam as our enemy. On August 2, 2010, Rudy Giuliani spoke on the Jeff Katz radio show about the proposed building of a mosque near the site of the World Trade Center. Giuliani said, "They died there because of Islamic extremist terrorism. They are our enemy." Giuliani, who rallied the nation as it responded to the horrific terror attacks of 9/11, has painful firsthand experience. But is this the appropriate response for the Church? Too often we feel threatened by Islam, not because of a true threat, but simply because it is different and unknown.

As the gospel spread throughout the world during what is called the Great Century of Christian Missions, it appeared to leapfrog over Muslim lands because of the people's resistance. The conquest of previously Christian lands, Muslim rejection of the deity of Christ, and the minority status of Christian communities in Muslim countries have caused many people to conclude that Muslims are indeed the enemy of the gospel. But an examination of the Scriptures shows this is not so. The only enemy we have is Satan.

New Testament writers use two different words that are commonly translated "enemy." Passages such as, *Love your neighbor and hate your enemy* (Matthew 5:43) use the Greek word *echthros* from *échthos* which means "to be hostile toward, or at enmity with someone." But a different Greek word is used in I Peter 5:8 where we read, *"Your enemy the devil prowls around like a roaring lion looking for someone to devour.*" Here, enemy is better translated as "adversary" (*antidikos* from *anti* meaning "against" and *dike* meaning "a cause or suit at law"). *Antidikos* was originally used in reference to an opponent in a lawsuit (see Matthew 5:25; Luke 12:58; 18:3). Later it came to mean an adversary or enemy that had nothing to do with legal affairs. An adversary is one who contends with, opposes, or resists.

History is filled with examples of Muslim hostility towards Christians. It is also filled with examples of our enmity towards them. But it's crucial that we keep in mind that our only true adversary is Satan. It is he who accuses us before God. Islam is a tool used to lead people away from Christ or prevent them from coming to Him, but so are Hinduism, Buddhism, secularism, capitalism, communism, and so forth. All these false systems are enemies, but the Devil alone is our adversary.

We are instructed to pray for our enemies. Some are intentional in their hostility and others are unintentional. Either way, we must take care that we do not make them the "end" or cause of the problem. For our true adversary is one who is behind such an approach. It is right for us to oppose the Devil (our *antidikos*), but we are to respond with love towards our enemies (our *echthros*). By making Muslims out to be our adversary, we erect barriers that keep us from demonstrating God's great love for them. I know many Muslims, and I have great relationships with them. I can say from first-hand experience that not all Muslims persecute Christians. In fact, most do not. But all Muslims do need to hear the gospel, for that is the only way they can be reconciled with God. Satan works hard to derail God's kingdom. No matter how much Islam seems to increase in power, the gospel can never be defeated.

Lesson #5: The Lord can use anyone.

My theology radically changed when I learned this final lesson. I watched the way God worked through the lives of uneducated, simple people, and I saw something I hadn't expected: We don't need high education or material belongings to be used by God. Considering who and what I was when I began this mission journey, that should have been apparent to me! But our problem is that we look at the outward person and quickly decide how successful we think he or she will be. Then we determine whether or not that person is worthy of our financial support. Oh, that we might look at others through God's eyes! *"The LORD does not look at the things people look at. People look at the outward appearance, but the LORD looks at the heart."* (I Samuel 16:7).

In remote villages around the globe, sitting in houses with leaky roofs far away from the modern world, are men and women filled with the same Holy Spirit that is in Billy Graham or the Apostle Paul. Think about it. The very same Holy Spirit, and in the exact same amount. God is every bit as present in what they are doing as He is in our most vibrant preachers and evangelists. We might think there isn't much hope for their kind, but God doesn't agree. He is using them right now, and He's doing it in extraordinary ways.

So there you have it, the story I have to tell and the lessons I learned along the way. But the real story is far from finished. Millions of Sundanese have yet to hear the gospel message. They are still waiting to experience the love of Christ through the witness of His people. You can do something about that. As you seek the Lord's guidance, ask Him, "Lord, what would You have my part in this to be?" It's an important question, because now it is your turn to write the rest of the story of

God's work in West Java. Or perhaps in some other place. But this much is for certain: God does want to use you. He wants you to commit yourself completely into His hands. And, really, there is no better place to be.

Made in the USA
Charleston, SC
12 November 2013